Everyday FOLK

Over 175 folk embroidery
designs for the home, inspired
by traditional textiles

Krista West

DAVID & CHARLES
—PUBLISHING—

www.davidandcharles.com

CONTENTS

Introduction

For many thousands of years, human beings have been fascinated by ornamenting themselves and their environs, from prehistoric forays into body art and cave paintings, to the intricately woven tunic banding embellishments of the ancient world; from the lavish tapestries of medieval Europe, to our ongoing enchantment with fashion and home decoration—in every environment we have found ourselves, we seek to adorn and decorate, whether it's a warrior painted for battle, a courtier dressed in the latest fashion, or a barista sporting her newest tattoo.

The Start of My Crafting Journey

In childhood, I experimented with sewing, crochet, knitting, and embroidery. As a young adult in the 1980s, I was introduced to cross stitch embroidery but found the then-popular sentimental designs too cloying and insubstantial for my taste, gravitating instead towards handcrafts with more historic depth. I dabbled in Amish hand-quilting, American Deerfield embroidery, and Fair Isle knitting, and developed a love for the geometric, stylized, and repeating designs that seemed to make up so much of historical craft.

When I had the opportunity in my early twenties to apprentice to a master ecclesiastical tailor, to learn to make Greek Orthodox liturgical garments and paraments, I made the decision to forego college and pursue life as a craftsperson. During the day I would measure, cut, and fit elaborate brocades; and in the evenings, I would unwind with my current knitting or embroidery project.

It was my tailoring work that first took me to Greece in 2005, as I sought to research traditional liturgical vesture and infuse my practice with the aesthetics of the Byzantine world. Many subsequent trips followed, as I searched for authentic brocades and finishings. It was on one such trip that I made an incredible discovery that was to take my crafting in a new direction.

A Discovery in Athens

I was sitting in the office of Dimitri, my mill agent in central Athens, waiting my turn to place an order and stitching a small embroidery project to pass the time, when—pointing to my embroidery—he asked if I wanted to see more? I nodded enthusiastically as he started walking out of his office, motioning to me to come. I jogged to keep up as he took me through the twists and turns of several busy blocks, ending up in a crowded commercial area next to an unassuming shop door. "Go," he said, leaving me there.

Walking in, I saw a small section of knitting yarn with a few European knitwear posters, then a shelf with some bolts of fabric, and at the back of the shop, some hanks of embroidery floss and metallic threads. "Oh," I thought, "a neighborhood craft store." I was about to turn on my heel and catch up with Dimitri, anxious that I wouldn't be able to find my way back to his office, when the shop owner pointed to a table with a large three-ring binder on it. To be polite, I headed over and began to turn its pages, full of sentimental cross stitch designs; to be respectful, I continued, discovering, to my surprise, a grainy photo of a gloriously intricate cross stitch design, featuring stylized florets set within a meandering pattern. Clearly Byzantine in style, with the unique and compelling tension between restraint and abundance that so marks that art, the red stitches outlined with black were so simple and yet so complex, creating an embroidery that truly felt like a work of art.

More Where That Came From

Turning the page, there was another equally compelling design, and so it went on—grainy photo after grainy photo of the most fabulous, geometric designs. I had no idea the cross stitch I had turned my nose up at as a young adult could be like this. The shop owner heard me gasp and said, "Oh, you like? Look under." On the shelves beneath were at least 20 more binders, all filled with "traditional" designs. She asked if I wanted to see the traditional fabrics and colors, too, and went on to introduce me to Greek folk embroidery with its unique evenweave fabrics and vibrant Mediterranean color palette of rich reds, deep blues, and warm golds. Three hours later, I'd loaded up on so many supplies, I had to buy a suitcase from a sidewalk vendor to get it all back to my hotel!

Visiting a friend in Thessaloniki the following week, I asked about the "traditional" embroidery, so he took me to his mother, Evi, who happily brought out her prized "*prika*" (heirloom embroideries passed from generation to generation). I marveled at the stylized motifs, and how every piece was made to be used and appreciated in everyday life—tiny table mats, large table runners, cushion covers, squares of all sizes. Evi showed me a beautiful basketweave design that she had learned in elementary school. I quickly made a sketch and began stitching on the plane ride home.

Inspired to Stitch

Returning home with my suitcase full of traditional supplies and patterns, I continued stitching all sorts of embroideries for my own home—large squares of linen with intricate red and black borders, table runners with small repeating motifs in teal and copper (so mid-century modern!), and terra cotta and gold cushion covers that my kids snuggled up to while watching TV. I loved how these timeless designs gave our rooms a warm, lived-in feel. They all seemed to "go" with each other, no matter the color palette or motif—I could set a runner with a Byzantine meander on a table, next to a chair with a cushion embroidered with an Ionian floral design, and they just looked happy together. It was so easy, yet so beautiful.

It was this discovery of the practical coziness of folk embroidery that started me on my journey to share folk embroidery with the world. Studying photos I had taken in Greece, or those shared by friends of the embroideries of their mothers and grandmothers, I had to heavily adapt them with design software to figure out missing elements, add corners, and arrange them for the finished size piece I wanted. Friends in Greece sent me books on folk embroidery, and I discovered that I loved bringing the old designs into new formats and color palettes, and so I began designing every chance I could get.

Avlea Folk Embroidery

I opened my business in late 2017 with just three small kits, thinking this would be a great hobby business when I retired from tailoring. But word spread—there was an enthusiastic interest in folk embroidery and it seemed I wasn't alone in asking that perennial question upon finishing a project, "What do I do with it?" So I found myself developing more historically-inspired designs for a growing community of makers who wanted patterns that were both useful and beautiful.

The clarion call of folk embroidery is "Use it!", and I've been delighted to watch stitchers across the world embrace its stunningly beautiful yet utterly practical nature. I see my work as a translator of sorts, helping makers everywhere discover traditional folk embroidery in a format that is easy and accessible, whether it's a small, embroidered motif for a tote bag, or a complex table runner stitched as a family heirloom. My creative curiosity has led me beyond the folk embroidery of Greece to that of many countries, including Latvia, Romania, Serbia, Hungary, Ukraine, Italy, and Asia Minor, and I continue to be fascinated by the shared designs and motifs across these diverse lands.

But what brings me the greatest sense of purpose in my work is the community of folk embroidery stitchers who are reviving this glorious and beautiful craft tradition. In the historic Byzantine understanding of craft, craftspeople are seen as "links in a chain," handing down knowledge and skill, generation to generation. It is understood to be both an honor and a responsibility to keep the traditions alive, and I feel deep joy and gratitude to play my part in sharing this historical textile art with others.

The Creative Power of Ornamentation

Every successive era has brought us a treasure trove of aesthetic styles, each with a distinctive look and feel, each adding another expression to the great canon of human creativity. While it is easy to see the grand masterpieces and be dazzled by their majesty, there is another very human story told in the objects that have been crafted for daily household use, and embellished with colors, patterns, and symbols, an undertaking that, on the face of it, is wholly unnecessary—after all, plain cloth is just as useful as embroidered cloth—yet we find ourselves drawn to the vibrant work of decorating cloth in every generation. While the modern era has seen aesthetic trends of minimalism and austere environments with very little adornment, design trends always seem to circle back to embellishment and ornamentation.

I believe this desire to ornament the textiles that surround us in our daily lives is a means of practicing our fundamental need to be creative. While we may not have the skill to make a grand painting or towering sculpture for our homes, we can quite easily pick up a needle and thread and create a wonderland of contrast, texture, and intricacy in something as simple as a pillow or a table runner. And, we can enjoy this beautiful work of our hands in the humblest of homes. We don't need to live in a country manor or a chic condo to be able to delight in color and pattern.

The Comfort of Textiles

On my very first trip to Greece, I stayed in a rooming house in a small village on the island of Crete. The room was spartan—white walls, twin beds, wooden chair—but my bed was covered with a stunning handwoven Greek blanket and the windows were hung with white cotton curtains finished with embroidered borders. These two small adornments made the room feel both cozy and luxurious; I came away from that trip with a renewed sense of the power of textiles to help us inhabit our spaces in a way that brings both comfort and delight.

A few years later, it came time for my family to move from the home we had lived in for almost a decade. I couldn't move the walls I had painted or the bathroom I had remodeled, but I could take my embroidered table runners, squares, and cushion covers. As we unpacked boxes, I came to appreciate the practical portability of textiles: I set out my prized table squares and tossed cushion covers on the sofa, and within moments this new house felt "ours." Scholars have long observed the practicality and ease of transporting textiles—mosaic designs created in the 6th century in Ravenna in Italy are thought to have been inspired in part by silk scraps the mosaicists carried with them—and I learned this afresh in the 21st century as I embellished our new home with our old textiles.

Your Folk Embroidery Journey Awaits

So, while folk embroidery has a long and storied history, it also has an inspiring future ahead. It's an easy skill to pick up and you can surround yourself in bright colors and compelling designs no matter where life takes you. There is a wonderful creative journey awaiting you as you explore these historic designs and decide how you will use them in new ways, whether it's stitching a small banding for a tote bag to bring a little folk charm out into the world with you, or creating a new heirloom to be cherished for decades to come.

This is the power of folk embroidery as it winds its way through the years, being rediscovered and reimagined in each generation, then passed on to the next. These beautiful textiles are a vibrant reminder of the creative, imaginative power that lies within all of us. A power that we can experience every day as we ornament our environments with these dazzling designs and lively colors.

Welcome to the journey!

Krista

Tools and Materials

While there are a variety of embroidery techniques used in traditional folk embroidery, this book focuses on the one most often encountered—perhaps because it is so easy to learn—and that is the counted thread embroidery technique of cross stitch. It is typically stitched on an evenweave (counted thread) fabric using six-strand cotton embroidery floss. With just a few tools and some fabric and floss, you can begin making beautiful folk embroidery pieces in no time!

TOOLS

There are only a few essential tools required to make your cross stitch folk embroideries. A hoop, a tapestry needle, and a pair of scissors are all you need to get started.

Hoops and QSnaps

The use of an embroidery hoop or frame makes the fabric taut and this will help you to keep your stitch tension even.

A 6in (15.5cm) beechwood hoop is a great basic hoop. It is easy to transport, very affordable, and widely available at your local craft shop or online. QSnaps are another option. These are sections of rigid plastic tubing that you wrap your work around, using the accompanying plastic clamps to "snap" it in place, hence the name!

If you are stitching for longer sessions or have fatigue issues, or want to stitch with both hands, you can invest in an embroidery stand. These come in a variety of styles and sizes but my personal preference is the Lowery workstand as it is extremely stable and durable. You simply clamp your embroidery hoop or QSnaps in place, leaving you free to stitch with either your dominant hand only, or both hands together. Other types available include stands that can be held on the lap, clamped to a table edge, or set on any type of work surface.

Needles

To work your counted thread folk embroidery you will need a tapestry needle (also known as a "cross stitch needle"). This type of needle has a blunt end which makes it perfectly suited to the stitching technique since you are going between the threads of fabric, rather than piercing through them.

Tapestry needles come in multiple sizes, and the higher the number of the needle, the finer it will be. I recommend starting with a size 24 tapestry needle, which works well for counted thread fabrics with a thread count of between 26-count and 32-count (see Materials: Fabrics), and the eye of the needle is large enough that it is easy to thread with two strands of embroidery floss (if you use a lower number needle, the eye is smaller and will be harder to thread). I have used a John James size 24 tapestry needle for all projects in this book.

To finish your work with the drawn thread hem technique, you will also need an embroidery (sharp) needle and I recommend John James size 7 embroidery (sharp) needles for this.

Additional Items

Thimble—Some people like to work with a thimble, but it's entirely a matter of personal preference. If you want to give it a go, I recommend a quilter's thimble, which has a concave top. They come in various sizes so you may need to try a few to find the fit you like.

Scissors—A small pair of embroidery snips is all you need while you're stitching. A larger pair of sewing shears is helpful for trimming and finishing your completed embroidery, but not absolutely necessary.

Floss organizers—These small pieces of cardboard or plastic are very handy for keeping your floss neat and organized when stitching. The ones on my website have a large hole to store your floss in and a smaller hole for attaching to a binder clip, although there are many different types available.

Thread conditioner—Some people like to use thread conditioner to keep their floss tangle-free. You can also use a piece of beeswax and lightly run each length of floss over it before you begin stitching.

Project bag—I recommend storing your project in a cotton bag between work sessions. This protects your work from dust, dirt, and mishaps. Alternately, you can wrap it in a clean kitchen towel.

Sewing thread—For working the drawn thread hem finish or making your embroidery into a project as described in Finishing Techniques, use a basic sewing thread in a color to match your fabric.

Magnifying glasses—If you think you won't be able to stitch on the finer threads of the evenweave fabrics used for folk embroidery designs, think again. A good pair of inexpensive magnifiers is all you need! However, if you wear glasses, then I recommend taking your embroidery with you to your next optometry visit: show your optometrist the distance at which you hold your work while stitching as they can adjust the focal distance of your eyeglass prescription and even prescribe specialty magnifiers just for stitching.

Lighting—You can use a simple task lamp or floor lamp to give you additional light as needed when stitching. While there are lots of craft-specific task lighting options available, any good source of light will do.

MATERIALS

Here, we'll take a look at what your choices are for fabric to stitch on to and threads to stitch with, to create a piece of counted thread folk embroidery with an authentic vibe.

Fabrics

In most folk embroidery, evenweave fabric—also known as counted thread fabric—is used. It is woven with an equal number of threads in both the warp and the weft to create a fabric that measures the same in either direction. The fabric thread count (abbreviated to "ct") indicates the number of threads per inch (per 2.5 centimeters). For example, a 30ct fabric has 30 threads in the warp (vertical direction) and 30 threads in the weft (horizontal direction), while a 26ct fabric has 26 threads in each direction, so the higher the count, the finer the fabric will be. All designs in this book are stitched over two threads in each direction (also known as stitching "over two"), so using a 30ct fabric results in 15 stitches to the inch (2.5cm), while using a 26ct fabric results in 13 stitches to the inch (2.5cm). (This information becomes important when making the folk embroidery designs your own, as explored in the Design Library.)

The traditional evenweave fabrics used give folk embroidery much of its distinctive appearance. Modern reproductions of these fabrics, produced in small batches in family-owned mills in Greece, are made on mechanized looms but in such a way as to preserve the character and texture of the historically handwoven fabrics—some even have slightly different numbers of threads in the warp or the weft to retain their characteristic unevenness. Counted thread linen fabrics, however, which are milled throughout Europe and more widely available in the US, tend to have more regular threads than traditional cotton evenweave fabrics, and this is because most of the evenweave linen fabrics available are made for modern cross stitch designs, in which regularity of threads is preferred.

A note about Aida cloth: Aida is a popular cross stitch fabric woven in blocks to give obvious holes, making it easy to see where to make each stitch. While Aida cloth can be substituted for any fabric specified in this book, it will not give the same folk texture as those specified.

Choosing your fabric

The choice of the fabric for your folk embroidery is part of the creative process. While all the projects in this book have a suggested fabric, you can substitute another to achieve a different effect, selected from the most common traditional fabrics used in the Mediterranean as the descriptions that follow: for example, you may like the wheat color and thicker texture of traditional ground cloth for a tote bag pocket, but prefer the smooth finish and crisp white of Mikini for a table square. Or you might want to splurge on more expensive linen for an heirloom table runner or a special wall hanging. When planning your project, think about your desired outcome. It's helpful to ask yourself the following questions:

1. What kind of texture would I like my finished embroidery to have?

- ✳ If you want a smooth finish, choose a mercerized cotton like Mikini 30ct

- ✳ If you want a handwoven-like texture, choose a more textured fabric such as traditional ground cloth 26ct

- ✳ If you want something in-between, choose linen

2. How would I like the color of the evenweave fabric to work with my design?

- ✳ If you would like to show off the design, particularly if working with bright colors, choose white, off-white, or ivory fabrics

- ✳ If you would like the fabric to bring a warm effect, choose natural or undyed fabrics

- ✳ If you would like to have a high contrast with the design, choose colored linens

A note about fabric care and preparation: Pre-washing is not recommended for evenweave fabrics as it can make the threads take up slightly, making them harder to see when stitching. After your embroidery is complete, most of these fabrics are best washed by hand in cool water with a gentle soap or detergent.

Traditional ground cloth, 100% cotton, 26ct

Traditional ground cloth (known as *archaveeto* in Greek) is made of 100% cotton threads with 26 threads in either direction, although because it is milled to mimic handwoven fabrics of the 17th and 18th centuries, it can have a slightly lower stitch count in one direction, so make sure to test stitch. It has a lovely soft hand with an almost plush texture, and is very easy to stitch because the threads are easy to see, making it a great choice for the beginner stitcher. It comes in a natural, undyed color, as well as a bright white.

Traditional ground cloth is great when you want durability and washability as it can be machine washed on a cold delicate cycle, making it ideal for table mats, table runners, table squares, and cushion covers. It will "full" slightly over time, which means that the threads will shrink a tiny bit and create an even more textured finish, highly desirable to folk embroidery enthusiasts.

A note about test stitching: Before you begin your project, produce a 1in (2.5cm) row of stitches in *each* direction and calculate your fabric size accordingly. When in doubt, allow an extra 15% fabric than the pattern stats specify.

Mikini, 100% cotton, 30ct (mercerized) and 26ct

Mikini fabric (known as *Mycinae* in Greek) is made of 100% cotton threads and I'd recommend both types as follows:

Mikini, 30ct mercerized—In the mercerization process, the cotton threads are treated with alkaline to improve the fabric's ability to receive dyes, increase its strength, reduce shrinkage, and give it a smooth, crisp finish. It is good for finer work, such as table runners and table squares, as it has excellent stitch definition. It has a soft hand and is pleasant to work with, and shows off drawn thread work beautifully. It comes in white and ivory.

Mikini, 26ct—This is not mercerized and therefore a little softer than Mikini 30ct, making it ideal for banding embellishments for clothes as well as for cushion covers and table squares. If traditional ground cloth is the folksy country cousin, then Mikini 26ct is the polished city cousin; but it, too, is very easy to work on as the threads are easy to see and count. It comes in two colors, white and ivory.

Linen, 100% linen, 30ct and 32ct

Linen for counted thread embroidery is made of 100% linen threads and is widely available in many different stitch counts (28ct, 30ct, 32ct, 36ct, 48ct, etc.)—I'd recommend 30ct and 32ct for your folk embroideries.

There are a wide range of colors to choose from, including many hand-dyed options—from warm taupe to saturated red to deep navy to darkest black and everything in-between—giving you an excellent choice when you want to create an embroidery that has more color and/or contrast.

A note about colorfastness: If you need to be able to launder your embroidery, always confirm your linen is colorfast before beginning to stitch, particularly if using a hand-dyed linen. Colorfast linens can be washed by hand; non-colorfast linen cannot be laundered as the dyes will bleed.

Lining and finishing fabrics

Some of the projects in this book, such as cushion covers and drawstring bags, require additional fabrics for making up the projects. Good-quality quilting cottons work very well for linings in particular, although home décor-type fabrics, or even vintage and repurposed fabrics, can be used to bring more textile interest to cushion backings.

Whether you choose to use solid-colored cotton or linen, or to opt for a patterned, home décor-type fabric, when selecting finishing fabrics, choosing colors or prints that harmonize with your embroidery design is another way to get creative.

A note about finishing fabric preparation: For items that will be laundered, it is recommended to pre-wash your lining fabric.

Floss, Threads, and Wools

Historically, folk embroideries were most often worked with silk floss (both twisted and untwisted) that had been dyed with natural pigments such as madder and indigo. However, with the advent of synthetic dyestuffs in the late 19th century, Greek needleworkers came to favor DMC six-strand cotton embroidery floss, as it was far less expensive and much more reliably colorfast, making it suitable for projects destined to be used in the home that needed occasional laundering. The projects in this book call for DMC floss for the same reasons.

DMC floss

DMC floss (also known as stranded cotton) is a 100% cotton thread made from six easily divisible strands (two strands are used when working the stitches in my designs). Colorfast, durable, and available in a wide array of colors, it is an excellent choice. For this book, I have created a palette of 14 colors inspired by classic Mediterranean hues but with slightly softer shades that harmonize better with modern interiors, and these are listed here:

3787 brown grey dark—A color like faded ink that is a softer option to a classic 310 black

3032 mocha brown medum—A soft taupe

469 avocado green—A warm green

3012 khaki green medium—A warm light green

730 olive green very dark—A deep olive-brown

733 olive green medium—A rich green-gold

598 turquoise—A bright turquoise

3810 turquoise dark—A deep, intense turquoise

924 grey green very dark—A deep, warm blue

926 grey green medium—A medium, warm blue

21 light alizarin—A soft coral

355 terra cotta dark—A rich, warm red

815 garnet—A bright burgundy

3857 rosewood dark—A deep burgundy-brown

A note about skein lengths: DMC floss comes in skeins of 8.7yd (8m).

Crewel wool

As an alternative to DMC floss, folk embroidery designs can be worked using crewel wool, a single-strand 2ply yarn that provides a soft, cozy texture perfect for home décor items, especially cushion covers.

Crewel wool is available from several companies, but I recommend Appletons crewel wool due to its durability and colorfastness. Skeins are sold in lengths of 27.3yds (25m), and you will need to allow for three times the yardage/meterage of crewel wool when substituting it for DMC floss. If you wish to substitute Appletons crewel wool for any of the designs in this book, color conversion tables are easily available online, but as wool dyes differently from cotton, substitutions will not be an exact match.

When choosing a design to stitch with crewel wool, I advise you to select one that is more open and that does not have a lot of fill stitches. Crewel wool has greater loft and texture than cotton embroidery floss, so a design with more unstitched areas will better bring out that cozy texture. Choose a design without any fabric showing through and the resulting embroidery can look more like needlepoint than folk embroidery!

A note about laundering: Wool-stitched embroideries should only ever be washed by hand.

Silk floss

Stranded silk floss can be substituted for any of the designs and each manufacturer will have a conversion chart for substituting their product for DMC six-strand cotton embroidery floss. However, silk flosses are rarely colorfast. If you want to launder your embroidery, I recommend stitching a small test area on scrap fabric and then hand-washing to see if the silk floss dyes bleed.

Getting Started

Now we have explored the tools and materials you will need, let's review the stitching process itself, including finding your start point, working your cross stitch embroidery from a charted design, and finishing off your stitching neatly. Then you'll be ready to get started on one of the 14 essential projects provided to begin your folk embroidery journey.

Step One: Choose Fabric and Floss

Choose your fabric—Each project provides a suggested fabric with a specific stitch count. If you choose to substitute a fabric with a higher stitch count, your stitched design will work up smaller. If you choose to substitute a fabric with a lower stitch count, your stitched design will work up larger.

Choose your floss—DMC six-strand cotton embroidery floss has been used for almost all the projects, with the exception of the Evian Terrazzo Cushion Cover, which uses Appletons crewel wool. The list of colors used for the stitched designs is provided with the quantity of skeins required for working on the fabric count specified. Where less than one skein is required it is indicated like this: (<1 skein). If you have chosen to work on a fabric with a different stitch count from the one used, you may need a little less or a little more floss. And remember, if you choose to substitute Appletons crewel wool for any project, you need to allow three times the yardage/meterage (i.e. 1yd/1m of DMC floss = 3yds/3m of Appletons crewel wool).

Step Two: Prepare to Stitch

Prepare your floss—Cut your DMC floss into 24–36in (60–90cm) lengths and store the colors on your floss organizers. Take a piece of cut floss, separate out two strands and thread these through your tapestry needle (if using Appletons crewel wool, use a single strand).

Mark your start position—Lay out your fabric on a flat surface and mark where to begin stitching as stated in the project instructions, most often with either a corner start (diagram A) or a center start (diagram B). With your threaded needle, pull a bit of floss through your fabric to mark your start point and trim, leaving a 3in (7.5cm) tail.

Hoop up your fabric—Place your fabric over the bottom section of the hoop (the smooth one without the screw), then position the top section over the fabric, sandwiching the fabric in between, making sure your marked start point is within the hoop. Tighten the screw slightly, then pull your fabric taut all around the hoop, continuing to tighten the screw until you reach your desired tension. If you are a beginner, I recommend a medium level of tension—not too tight, not too loose. As you stitch, you will discover your preferred tension and can adjust accordingly. You will need to repeat the tightening process occasionally as you are stitching.

Corner Start

To start at the corner, measure 2in (5cm) in from each corner and mark start position at dot as shown.

A

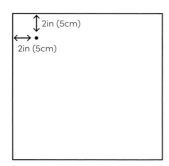

Center Start

To start in the center, mark the center spot by folding the fabric in half horizontally, then vertically.

B

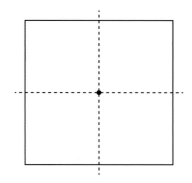

Step Three: Begin Stitching

Reading the charts—For each of the projects, the design to be stitched is shown on a grid and this is referred to as a "chart." Each square on the chart is printed with both a color and a symbol (this is called an SOC chart, or "symbol on color"), and the chart key tells you what color to work for each colored symbol. The charts in this book use letters as the symbols and these symbols are helpful when you have two shades of a similar color so you can tell them apart. Each square on the chart equals two threads horizontally and vertically on your fabric. This is called "stitching over two."

Working the cross stitches—For each cross stitch, you will work one diagonal stitch from left to right over two threads of the fabric, then one diagonal stitch from right to left, again over two threads of the fabric, to complete the stitch. Oftentimes, you'll be working several stitches of the same color in a particular area of your design and when that's the case, you can stitch all the left-leaning stitches to the end of that color section, then come back and stitch all the right-leaning stitches to complete a row of cross stitches (diagram C).

Chart pattern repeats—Most folk embroidery designs use a motif that is repeated multiple times to create the pattern. For the larger designs in the project chapters, like the Cerulean Scrolls Table Square for example, two charts are supplied: a close-up chart for ease of working shows the repeated motif, then you will need to refer to the full-size chart provided to see how many times to stitch that motif for your particular project. However, whenever space allows, full-size charts are included for the projects, so that you do not need to calculate the number of repeats to work.

Starting a thread—To begin stitching, pull your thread from the back of the fabric to the front, leaving about 1in (2.5cm) of floss on the back side of the fabric (this is the "tail"). Begin working the cross stitches from left to right, starting with the right-leaning diagonal stitches first and catching the tail beneath the first few stitches made to secure it (knots are not used in cross stitch because they will slip through counted thread fabrics).

Traveling a thread—If you need to "travel" the thread to another area of the design, you can simply start at the new position if it is fewer than five stitches away. If it is five or more stitches away, slip the floss through a couple of stitches on the back side of the fabric.

Finishing a thread—To finish stitching, slip the floss through five stitches on the back side of the fabric to secure, then trim.

....

Cross Stitch

Work diagonal stitches over two threads, first left to right, then right to left to complete the row.

C

ESSENTIAL INFORMATION

In addition to the charted design, your project chapter instructions also include the following information:

Size of stitched area—This is the area that your stitching will take up on the fabric (i.e. before you hem or finish it) if you use the fabric count recommended in the Supplies list; this is essential information to have if you plan to finish your embroidery in a different way from that shown, as you may need to add extra fabric at the planning stage (more about this in Design Library: Planning Your Folk Embroidery Project).

Stitch count—This is the number of stitches the design will cover. The number of stitches for the shorter side are listed first followed by the longer side. For example, for the Brindisi Diamonds Small Table Mat it looks like this:

STITCH COUNT: 107 x 143 sts/6395 total sts

This means that the design will be 107 stitches wide on the shorter side and 143 stitches long on the longer side. These are important numbers to know if you are going to substitute fabric of a larger or smaller count because you can use the stitch count to calculate how much fabric you will need. The total number of stitches (total sts) is the number of stitches that will be worked in the design: this can be helpful in determining how much time the design will take you to stitch.

Start position—This identifies where to start stitching on the fabric as explained in Getting Started—Step Two: Prepare to Stitch.

Finished size of project—This is the final size of the project when finished as shown.

Supplies—This lists the counted thread fabric used for the embroidery as shown, together with the DMC floss skein quantities in the colors required to stitch the design.

Finishing—Additional material requirements for making the project as shown are listed here, and you'll be referred to the Finishing Techniques section where you can find step-by-step instruction for turning your folk embroidery into the item pictured.

Embrace your imperfections

Lastly, a word of encouragement before you pick up your needle and thread...Folk embroidery has been made by thousands of people over thousands of years and many historic pieces feature "mistakes"—a stitch over the wrong thread, a wonky corner, a weird little motif to fill in a blank space. Instead of seeing these as mistakes, I prefer to view them as the perfect imperfection of something made by hand. While a machine can make something technically perfect, it does so with a soulless, lifeless quality, whereas making a thing by hand is a testament to our ability to adapt and accept a less-than-perfect state of affairs, and be transformed nonetheless. Embrace the imperfections in your work because they tell the story of your making hands!

....

Tip

If you are new to folk embroidery or want a smaller project, choose a smaller design. If you are an experienced stitcher and ready to take on a more involved project, choose a larger design.

Design Styles in Folk Embroidery

While folk embroidery is endlessly adaptable, it is helpful to divide the different design styles into categories. In this book, they are organized into six design styles that are shown used for a wide variety of household items and garments. Let's look at each design style in turn.

■ Allover Designs

These small, repeating motifs are a great example of those famous words of the ancient Greek philosopher, Aristotle—"the whole is greater than the sum of its parts." When a tiny geometric motif is stitched over and over again, something magical happens, and the resulting embroidery looks more complex and intricate than the single repeating motif. Allover designs—typically made as table mats, table runners, and cushion covers—are quite common in many of the countries that practice folk embroidery. The motifs vary widely, from simple repeating squares and diamonds to intricate stylized flowers and eight-pointed stars. While they can be worked in a single color, stitching with multiple colors will reveal delightful secondary motifs within the design for a more visually compelling design.

One of the great advantages of allover designs is that they lend themselves well to meditative stitching—once you get the first few motifs stitched, you can simply use those stitched motifs as your pattern, which makes them a great choice for travel, meetings, or any situation where you do not want to be constantly referring to a chart! These simple repeating motifs have the most modern feel of any of the folk embroidery design styles and suit almost any home décor, from mid-century modern to beach cottage.

Projects using allover designs are: Brindisi Diamonds Small Table Mat and Naxos Stars Mitered Cushion.

□ Perimeter Border Designs

Perimeter border designs are comprised of an intricately stitched design mirrored at each corner, extending around the entire outer edge of the fabric while the center remains unstitched, which creates a compelling negative space.

Most of these designs originate from the impressive towers of cushions displayed as status symbols in Greek homes of the 17th to 19th centuries, the lavishly embroidered borders peeking out from the edges of each cushion, with the centers not intended to be seen—a feast for the eyes with varying motifs and color palettes. A popular style for over three centuries, there are a wide variety of patterns to draw from—knotwork, diamonds, eight-pointed stars, vines, and floral motifs are all common. While historically most of these designs do not have corner motifs, today's charting software makes mirroring motifs easier.

A complex perimeter border design is often made up of two borders—a larger central border with a smaller, coordinating border worked on either one or both sides of it. This combination of smaller and larger motifs provides a great opportunity for creativity as the two borders can either harmonize or contrast.

Project using a perimeter border design is: Cerulean Scrolls Table Square.

◼ Centered Border Designs

In this design style, a wide border is stitched centered within the piece of fabric, and the space on either side of the border is left unstitched, creating a complex yet restrained look. It also allows for the use of wider, more complex borders that are too large to be worked as a perimeter border.

Centered border designs tend to be multi-directional, with the design being the same whether right-side up or upside-down. While perimeter and double-ended border designs are stitched from the corners of the fabric, centered border designs (like small border designs) are stitched from the center of the fabric outwards. This can be handy if you have miscalculated your fabric as you can simply stop when you get close to the raw edge of the fabric.

Typically used for either cushion covers or table runners, centered border designs vary in complexity from fairly simple, narrow borders to complex, wide borders. Like perimeter border designs, they are often comprised of a large central repeating motif flanked by a smaller border on either side, providing the same creative opportunity for the two borders to harmonize or contrast.

Projects using centered border designs are: Linden Leaves Table Runner, Thessaly Chevrons Table Runner, and Evian Terrazzo Cushion Cover.

☐ Double-Ended Designs

A double-ended design is a repeating motif that is mirrored at each end of a project. In the historic folk embroidery of the Greek islands, lavishly embroidered bed tent curtains were important household objects providing privacy and retaining warmth in the sleeping area, featuring intricate border designs made up of stylized flowers, urns, animals, figures, scrolls, geometric shapes, and myriad other motifs. Similarly stylized designs were also worked on the skirts of traditional folk costumes, as the voluminous fabric provided an excellent canvas to show off embroidery. Many such designs were adapted into table runners in the early 20th century and are a common sight in Greek homes today, on sideboards and coffee tables.

There are many beautiful designs to choose from and while they often look complicated, double-ended designs can be some of the fastest table runner patterns to work as the complex motifs are only worked at either end of the table runner, unlike perimeter designs which are stitched all the way around! They also allow for a nice amount of unstitched fabric in the center in which a plant, candle, or other decorative element can be displayed to great effect. Double-ended designs at either end of a rectangular table runner can be connected with a coordinating small outer border (typically 3–10 stitches wide), which makes counting to the other end of the table runner much easier.

Project using a double-ended design is:
Santorini Botanika Table Runner.

▪ Single Motif Designs

While all folk embroidery is made up of motifs—stars, diamonds, flowers, leaves, trees, urns, and so on—there are two traditions that utilize single motifs to great effect.

First is a group of dazzling designs that are made up of large, complex single motifs. Historically, these intricate designs were worked spaced apart in rows on large expanses of fabric to create magnificent bed tent curtains, most commonly from the Greek islands of Rhodes and Kos. Today, these exquisite motifs make a wonderful centerpiece for a wall hanging—or cushion cover—perfectly at home in a modern décor. Traditionally stitched in only one or two colors, you can choose to work these designs in their original simple color palettes, or add your own creative touch by using multiple colors.

The second type of single motif designs is made up of smaller units—typically a small square with some kind of design in the center—that are then generally repeated in a grid layout to create a larger design, resulting in a "tiled" effect. It is this that distinguishes them from the half-drop repeat format that is so common to allover designs.

Projects using single motif designs are: Dodecanese Ornamental Wall Hanging, Chrysanthy Geometric Cushion Cover, Odessa Tulips Cushion Cover, and Oak Leaves Drawstring Bag.

☐ Small Border Designs

Folk embroidery starts with just a single cross stitch, and many start their folk embroidery journey with the stitching of just a simple small border!

Embroiderers of the past used simple repeating units to create delightful small borders that were used on folk costumes and often paired with larger borders. While these small borders can be worked with a larger border (as is seen in perimeter border designs and centered border designs), they are endlessly versatile on their own, and they can be worked in pairs or groups to create ever new and fascinating designs. A friend in Greece once showed me an embroidered rug a Latvian friend of hers had stitched entirely out of small borders, yet the effect was visually striking and complex nevertheless.

With their smaller stitch repeat and simpler motifs, small borders are refreshingly easy to embroider—perfect for a little meditative stitching. They are also an ideal way to add just a hint of folk embroidery to another craft project, such as stitching a small band on a jacket pocket or as a trim for a child's dress.

Projects using small border designs are: Delphian Diamonds Envelope Bag, Cecille Border Drawstring Bag, and Primrose Banding Garment Trim.

IDENTIFY IT!

Look out for the symbol that identifies the type of design that has been used for each of the essential projects :

■ Allover Designs

☐ Perimeter Border Designs

▬ Centered Border Designs

▭ Double-Ended Designs

▣ Single Motif Designs

▢ Small Border Designs

ESSENTIAL PROJECTS

This section showcases 14 projects that are classic examples of folk embroidery design featuring the six different styles I've identified. If you are new to folk embroidery, they are a great place to start, as I have provided all the essential information you need so you can concentrate on the stitching. Do you enjoy the meditative quality of stitching an allover design, do you relish the complexity of a double-ended design, or do you favor a speedy small border design? Here's your opportunity to explore, and I'll introduce you to how these designs can be made into a range of beautiful items for your home.

BRINDISI DIAMONDS

Small Table Mat

■ This design is made up of simple diamonds connected by diagonal rows of stitching with small leaf motifs, to create a pattern reminiscent of mosaic tiles. Worked in two shades of olive green and two shades of madder red with a zigzag border, it is a terrific first project.

SIZE OF STITCHED AREA: 8¼ x 11in (21 x 28cm)
STITCH COUNT: 107 x 143 sts/6395 total sts
START POSITION: Corner start (see Getting Started)
FINISHED SIZE OF PROJECT: 10 x 13in (25.5 x 33cm)

Model stitched by Maria Armstrong. ▸▸▸

Supplies

◈ One piece of 26ct traditional ground cloth in natural, 13 x 16in (33 x 40cm)

◈ DMC Floss:
  730 olive green very dark, 16yds/14.6m (2 skeins)
  733 olive green medium, 8yds/7.3m (1 skein)
  21 light alizarin, 8yds/7.3m (1 skein)
  355 terra cotta dark, 6yds/5.5m (<1 skein)

Finishing

To finish as shown, follow instructions for the Drawn Thread Hem (see Finishing Techniques: Making Table Mats, Squares, and Runners), allowing for a 2in (5cm) hem allowance beyond the embroidery all around.

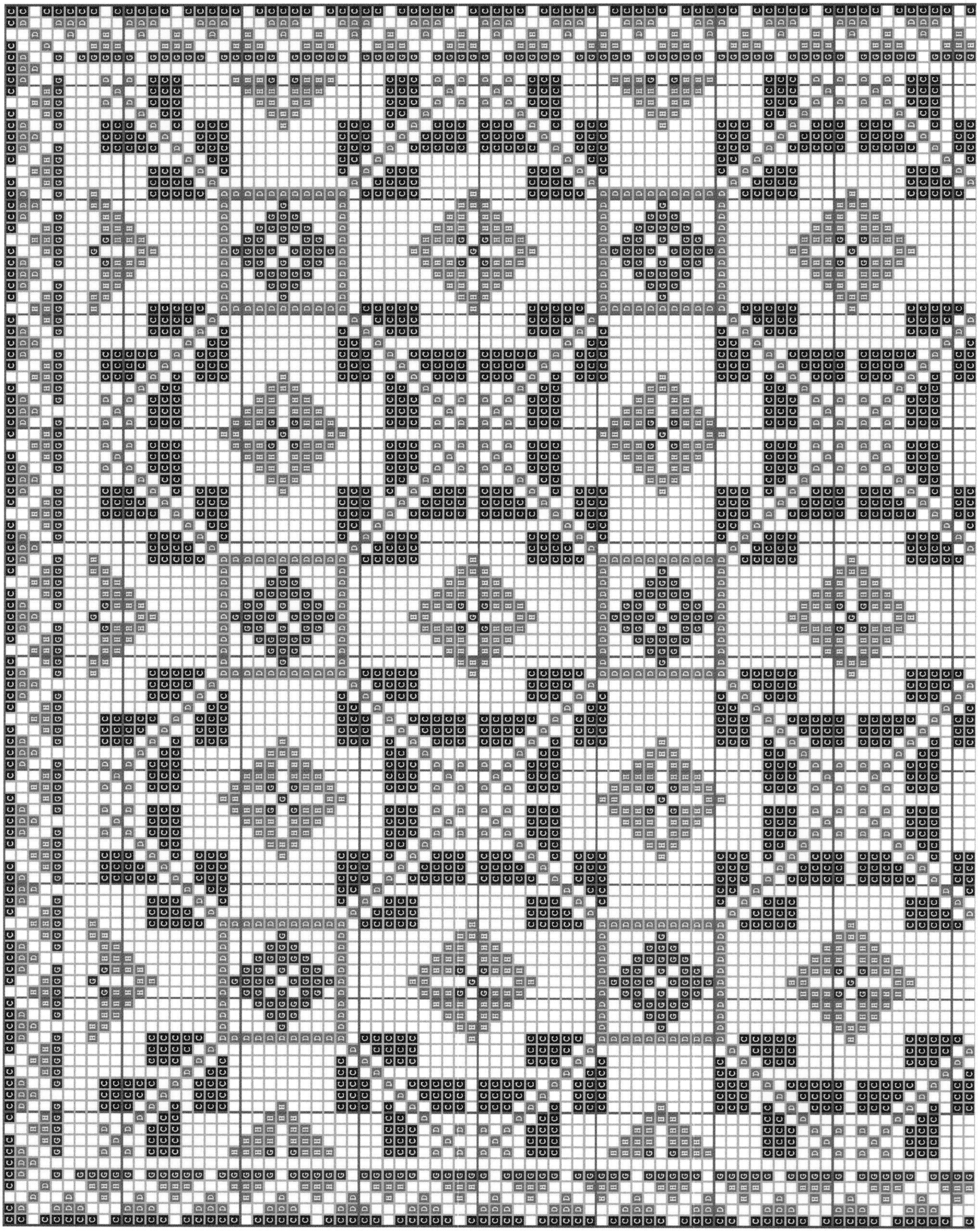

Key: Cross stitch
with 2 strands
....

C	DMC 730
D	DMC 733
G	DMC 355
H	DMC 21

NAXOS STARS
Mitered Cushion

■ The embroideries of the island of Naxos have a distinctive style of repeating star motifs. Traditionally two shades of red are used, but you can choose any light and dark floss color. This design is made as an inset for a cushion cover, but could be worked with additional repeats for a table square or table runner.

SIZE OF STITCHED AREA: 9 x 9in (23 x 23cm)
STITCH COUNT: 135 x 135 sts/11097 total sts
START POSITION: Corner start (see Getting Started)
FINISHED SIZE OF PROJECT: For an 18 x 18in (46 x 46cm) pillow form

Model stitched by Krista West. ▸▸

Supplies

◈ One piece of 30ct linen in off-white, 13 x 13in (33 x 33cm)

◈ DMC Floss:
355 terra cotta dark, 40yds/36.5m (5 skeins)
3857 rosewood dark, 20yds/18.3m (3 skeins)

Finishing

To finish as shown, you will need a ¼yd (0.25m) piece of border fabric, two pieces of backing fabric 13 x 19in (33 x 48cm), and an 18 x 18in (46 x 46cm) pillow form; follow instructions for the Cushion Cover with Mitered Borders (see Finishing Techniques: Making Cushion Covers).

**Key: Cross stitch
with 2 strands**

E DMC 3857
G DMC 355

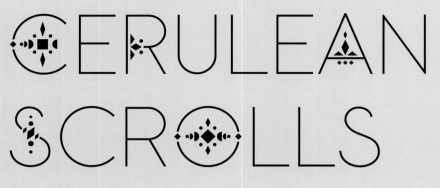

CERULEAN SCROLLS

Table Square

☐ This perimeter border design features a central border with a graceful scrolling vine motif connected by diagonal lines. The outer and inner borders are comprised of diamonds, echoing the diagonal lines of the central border. Worked in three shades of warm blue inspired by traditional indigo dyes, it is finished as a table square with a drawn thread hem, but could also be made into a cushion cover.

SIZE OF STITCHED AREA: 14⅛ x 14⅛in (36 x 36cm)
STITCH COUNT: 215 x 215 sts/14492 total sts
START POSITION: Corner start (see Getting Started)
FINISHED SIZE OF PROJECT: 16 x 16in (40.5 x 40.5cm)

Model stitched by Elizabeth Ostler. ▸▸▸

Supplies

◈ One piece of 30ct linen in off-white, 18 x 18in (46 x 46cm)

◈ DMC Floss:
  926 grey green medium, 38yds/34.7m (5 skeins)
  924 grey green very dark, 32yds/29.3m (4 skeins)
  598 turquoise light, 14yds/12.8m (2 skeins)

Finishing

To finish as shown, follow instructions for the Drawn Thread Hem (see Finishing Techniques: Making Table Mats, Squares, and Runners), allowing a 2in (5cm) hem allowance beyond the embroidery all around.

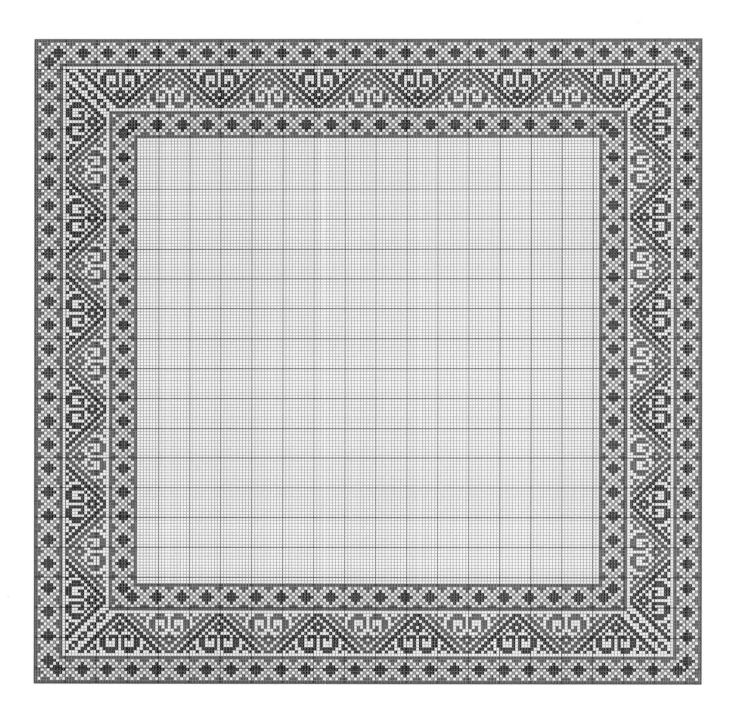

Key: Cross stitch
with 2 strands
....

I DMC 926
J DMC 598
K DMC 924

LINDEN LEAVES

Table Runner

This design features a classic Ukrainian motif, where mirrored pairs of scrolls create a diamond shape, but it is worked in a modern color palette of light and dark shades of warm blue. Shown finished as a table runner, it could also be made into a cushion cover.

SIZE OF STITCHED AREA: 4½ x 23½in (11.5 x 60cm)
STITCH COUNT: 67 x 353 sts/10993 total sts
START POSITION: Center start (see Getting Started)
FINISHED SIZE OF PROJECT: 10½ x 24in (27 x 61cm)

Model stitched by Maria Armstrong. ▶▶

Supplies

◈ One piece of 30ct linen in off-white, 13 x 28in (33 x 71cm)

◈ DMC Floss:
926 grey green medium, 40yds/36.5m (5 skeins)
924 grey green very dark, 24yds/22m (3 skeins)

Finishing

To finish as shown, follow instructions for the Drawn Thread Hem (see Finishing Techniques: Making Table Mats, Squares, and Runners), allowing for a hem allowance beyond the embroidery of 1in (2.5cm) on the short sides and 4in (10cm) on the long sides. Work drawn thread hem on long sides only; on the short sides, secure hem in place with whipstitch.

Key: Cross stitch
with 2 strands
....

K DMC 924
I DMC 926

THESSALY CHEVRONS

Table Runner

▬ Showcasing the serrated carnation motif common to many styles of folk embroidery, this design is worked in a classic palette of shades of red complemented with green. It is shown finished as a striking table runner with a drawn thread hem.

SIZE OF STITCHED AREA: 5¾ x 17in (15 x 43cm)
STITCH COUNT: 85 x 253 sts/12442 total sts
START POSITION: Center start (see Getting Started)
FINISHED SIZE OF PROJECT: 12 x 19in (30 x 48cm)

Model stitched by Cindy Russell. ▸▸

Supplies

◈ One piece of 30ct linen in off-white, 15 x 22in (38 x 56cm)

◈ DMC Floss:

355 terra cotta dark, 44yds/40m (5 skeins)

3857 rosewood dark, 23yds/21m (3 skeins)

21 light alizarin, 8yds/7.3m (1 skein)

3787 brown grey dark, 8yds/7.3m (1 skein)

733 olive green medium 8yds/7.3m (1 skein)

Finishing

To finish as shown, follow instructions for the Drawn Thread Hem (see Finishing Techniques: Making Table Mats, Squares, and Runners), allowing for a hem allowance beyond the embroidery of 2in (5cm) on the short sides and 4in (10cm) on the long sides.

**Key: Cross stitch
with 2 strands**

- **A** DMC 3787
- **E** DMC 3857
- **G** DMC 355
- **H** DMC 21
- **D** DMC 733

EVIAN TERRAZZO
Cushion Cover

■ This cross-cultural design features a Latvian-inspired central motif, flanked by a Ukrainian octagon border, and finished with a small Greek leaf border. It is worked in Appletons crewel wool and made into a cozy cushion cover.

SIZE OF STITCHED AREA: 5 x 15¼in (13 x 39cm)
STITCH COUNT: 63 x 197 sts/6142 total sts
START POSITION: Center start (see Getting Started)
FINISHED SIZE OF PROJECT: For a 16 x 16in (40.5 x 40.5cm) pillow form

Model stitched by Pamela Filbert. ▸▸

Supplies

◈ One piece of 26ct traditional ground cloth in natural, 18 x 18in (46 x 46cm)

◈ Appletons Crewel Wool:
2 skeins of 327 dull marine blue
2 skeins of 155 mid blue
1 skein of 313 brown olive

Finishing

To finish as shown, you will need two pieces of backing fabric 12 x 17in (30 x 43cm) and one 16 x 16in (40.5 x 40.5cm) pillow form; follow instructions for the Basic Cushion Cover (see Finishing Techniques: Making Cushion Covers).

Key: Cross stitch with 1 strand

....

- D Appletons 313
- K Appletons 327
- I Appletons 155

Reminder

For this design, I have used Appletons crewel wool so I have sitched with just a single strand of the yarn. If you choose to use DMC floss, don't forget that you will need to use two strands.

SANTORINI BOTANIKA

Table Runner

☐ This double-ended design features classic urns filled with stylized flowers, including carnations, bordered by a delicate row of connected diamonds. Worked on traditional ground cloth for a folk texture and finished with a drawn thread hem to create a table runner, there is a large unstitched central area for ornament display.

SIZE OF STITCHED AREA: 14¼ x 20⅛in (36.5 x 51cm)
STITCH COUNT: 187 x 259 sts/11484 total sts
START POSITION: Corner start (see Getting Started)
FINISHED SIZE OF PROJECT: 16½ x 22in (42 x 56cm)

Model stitched by Krista West. ▸▸▸

Supplies

◈ One piece of 26ct traditional ground cloth in natural, 19 x 24in (48 x 61cm)

◈ DMC Floss:
  3787 brown grey dark, 32yds/29.3m (4 skeins)
  355 terra cotta dark, 16yds/14.6m (2 skeins)
  733 olive green medium, 8yds/7.3m (1 skein)
  21 light alizarin, 6yds/5.5m (<1 skein)
  469 avocado green, 6yds/5.5m (<1 skein)
  3012 khaki green medium, 6yds/5.5m (<1 skein)
  815 garnet medium, 2yds/1.8m (<1 skein)
  598 turquoise light, 2yds/1.8m (<1 skein)

Finishing

Follow instructions for the Drawn Thread Hem (see Finishing Techniques: Making Table Mats, Squares, and Runners), allowing for a 2in (5cm) hem allowance.

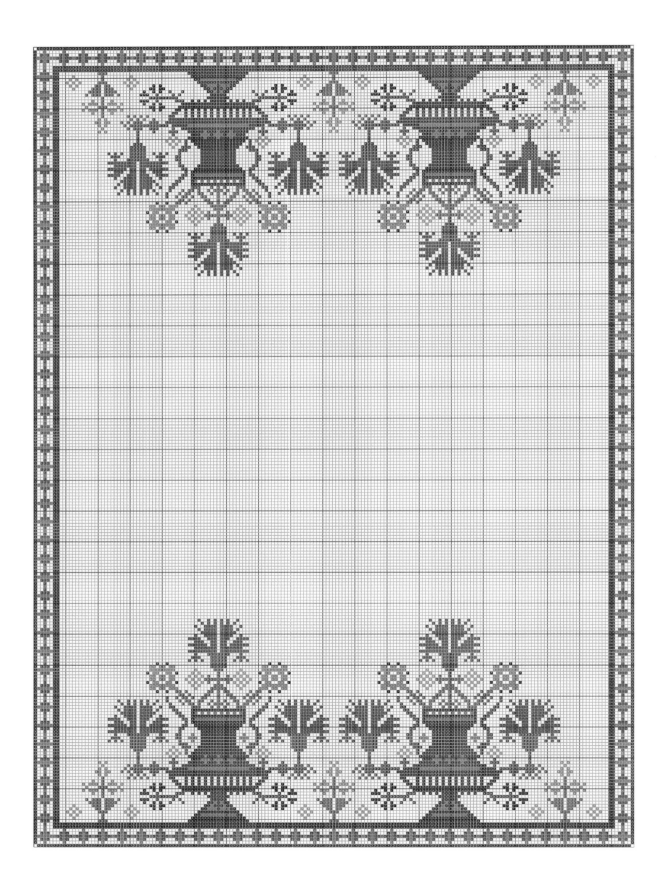

**Key: Cross stitch
with 2 strands**

....

- **A** DMC 3787
- **D** DMC 733
- **F** DMC 815
- **G** DMC 355
- **H** DMC 21
- **J** DMC 598
- **M** DMC 469
- **N** DMC 3012

DODECANESE ORNAMENTAL
Wall Hanging

◾ This intricate single motif design is inspired by a bed curtain valance from the Greek island of Kos. Finishing your embroidery as a wall hanging allows you to show off your stitching without the added expense of framing.

SIZE OF STITCHED AREA: 10½ x 8¾in (27 x 22cm)
STITCH COUNT: 139 x 169 sts/7884 total sts
START POSITION: Center start (see Getting Started)
FINISHED SIZE OF PROJECT: 13 x 9in (33 x 23cm)

Model stitched by Krista West. ▶▶▶

Supplies

◈ One piece of 32ct linen in ivory, 18 x 18in (46 x 46cm)

◈ DMC Floss:
469 avocado green, 40yds/36.5m (5 skeins)
926 grey green medium, 2yds/1.8m (<1 skein)

Finishing

To finish as shown, you will need one piece of lining fabric 18 x 18in (46 x 46cm) and a 12in (30cm) tapestry rod; follow instructions for Making a Wall Hanging (see Finishing Techniques).

Key: Cross stitch
with 2 strands
....

■ᴍ DMC 469
■ᴵ DMC 927

CHRYSANTHY GEOMETRIC

Cushion Cover

■ This design features a geometric pattern inspired by motifs from the Aegean island of Chios in the Mediterranean Sea. It is shown finished as a stylish cushion cover, but it would also make a great wall hanging.

SIZE OF STITCHED AREA: 8 x 8in (20 x 20cm)
STITCH COUNT: 105 x 105 sts/4053 total sts
START POSITION: Center start (see Getting Started)
FINISHED SIZE OF PROJECT: For an 18 x 18in (46 x 46cm) pillow form

Model stitched by Krista West. ▸▸▸

Supplies

◈ One piece of 26ct Mikini in ivory, 19 x 19in (48 x 48cm)

◈ DMC Floss:
   733 olive green medium, 14yds/12.8m (2 skeins)
   924 grey green very dark, 10yds/9.2m (2 skeins)
   926 grey green medium, 6yds/5.5m (<1 skein)

Finishing

To finish as shown, you will need two pieces of backing fabric 13 x 19in (33 x 48cm) and a 18 x 18in (46 x 46cm) pillow form; follow instructions for the Basic Cushion Cover (see Finishing Techniques: Making Cushion Covers).

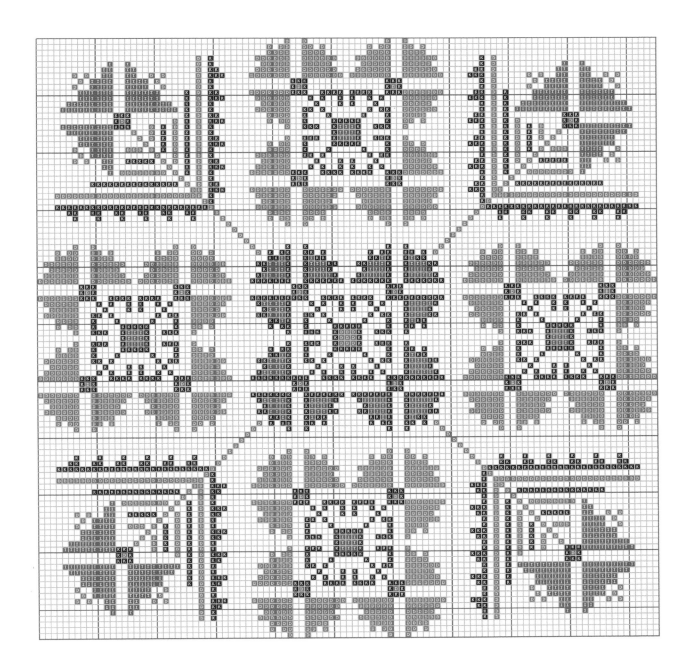

Key: Cross stitch
with 2 strands

K DMC 924
D DMC 733
I DMC 926

ODESSA TULIPS
Cushion Cover

■ This design showcases the beauty of repeating a single motif, such as these graceful tulips, which are found in the folk embroidery of many countries, including Ukraine.

SIZE OF STITCHED AREA: 7½ x 7½in (19 x 19cm)
STITCH COUNT: 109 x 109 sts/5680 total sts
START POSITION: Center start (see Getting Started)
FINISHED SIZE OF PROJECT: For a 14 x 14in (35.5 x 35.5cm) pillow form

Model stitched by Rachael Marks. ▶▶

Supplies

◈ One piece of 30ct linen in off-white, 15 x 15in (38 x 38cm)

◈ DMC Floss:

3857 rosewood dark, 10yds/9.2m (2 skeins)

355 terra cotta dark, 10yds/9.2m (2 skeins)

926 grey green medium, 10yds/9.2m (2 skeins)

924 grey green very dark, 5yds/4.6m (<1 skein)

Finishing

To finish as shown, you will need two pieces of backing fabric 10 x 15in (25.5 x 38cm) and a 14 x 14in (35.5 x 35.5cm) pillow form; follow instructions for the Basic Cushion Cover (see Finishing Techniques: Making Cushion Covers).

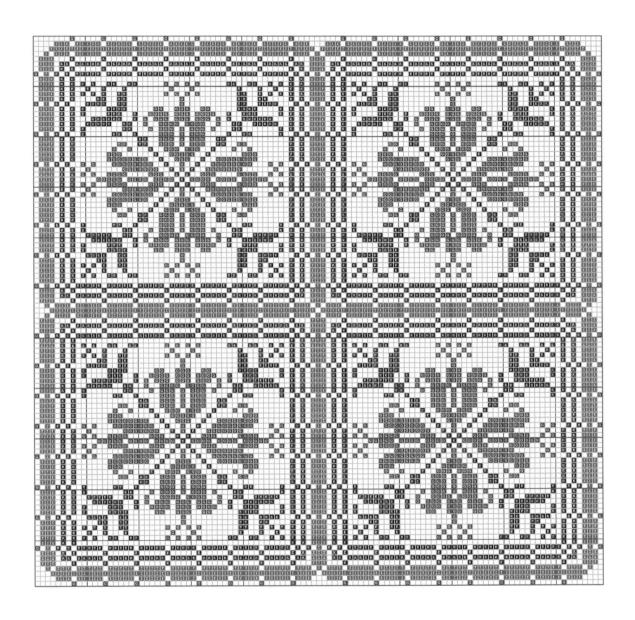

Key: Cross stitch
with 2 strands
....

G DMC 355
K DMC 924
E DMC 3857
I DMC 926

OAK LEAVES
Drawstring Bag

■ Here, delightful oak leaf corner motifs combine to create a peacock feather pattern at the centre of the design, an image often seen in the folk embroidery of many countries. Finished as a drawstring bag, you could stitch the alternative colorway provided in multiple repeats for a table runner or cushion cover.

SIZE OF STITCHED AREA: 4½ x 4½in (11.5 x 11.5cm)
STITCH COUNT: 57 x 57 sts/1601 total sts
START POSITION: Refer to Finishing Techniques: Making a Drawstring Bag (Oak Leaves diagram)
FINISHED SIZE OF PROJECT: 11½ x 9½in (29 x 24cm)

Model stitched by Krista West. ▸▸

Supplies

◈ One piece of 26ct traditional ground cloth in white, 10½ x 24in (26.5 x 60cm)

◈ DMC Floss:
  3012 khaki green medium, 5yds/4.6m (<1 skein)
  926 grey green medium, 4yds/3.7m (<1 skein)
  924 grey green very dark, 3yds/2.8m (<1 skein)

Finishing

To finish as shown, you will need one piece of lining fabric 10½ x 24in (26.5 x 60cm) and one drawstring cord 36in (91cm) long; follow instructions for Making a Drawstring Bag (see Finishing Techniques).

Key: Cross stitch
with 2 strands
....

I DMC 926
N DMC 3012
K DMC 924

ALTERNATIVE COLORWAY

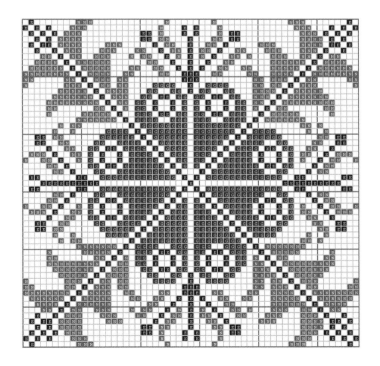

Key: Cross stitch
with 2 strands
....

G DMC 355
N DMC 3012
E DMC 3857

DELPHIAN DIAMONDS

Envelope Bag

☐ This design features at its center mirrored serrated borders that form large diamonds. Flanked by bands of small diamonds and stylized laurel leaf, this small border design can be made into an envelope bag for a tablet cover as shown, or as a table runner or cushion cover.

SIZE OF STITCHED AREA: 7½ x 9in (19 x 23cm)
STITCH COUNT: 97 x 117 sts/6022 total sts
START POSITION: Center start (see Getting Started)
FINISHED SIZE OF PROJECT: 11 x 9½in (28 x 24cm)

Model stitched by Debera Mahassos. ▶▶▶

Supplies

◈ One piece of 26ct Mikini in ivory, 12 x 14in (30 x 35.5cm)

◈ DMC Floss:
   733 olive green medium, 9yds/8.2m (2 skeins)

   3857 rosewood dark, 10yds/9.2m (2 skeins)

   355 terra cotta dark, 10yds/9.2m (2 skeins)

   730 olive green very dark, 4yds/3.7m (<1 skein)

   21 light alizarin, 2yds/1.8m (<1 skein)

   3810 turquoise dark, 3yds/2.8m (<1 skein)

Finishing

To finish as shown, you will need one piece of backing fabric 14 x 12in (35.5 x 30cm), one piece of lining fabric 24 x 12in (61 x 30cm), and one button; follow instructions for Making an Envelope Bag (see Finishing Techniques).

Key: Cross stitch
with 2 strands
....

C	DMC 730
D	DMC 733
E	DMC 3857
G	DMC 355
H	DMC 21
L	DMC 3810

CECILLE BORDER

Drawstring Bag

☐ This project showcases how a little folk embroidery can make a big impact. A graceful stylized floral border is finished as a handy drawstring bag, ideal for keeping your eyeglasses safe.

SIZE OF STITCHED AREA: 1¾ x 7½in (4.5 x 19cm)

STITCH COUNT: 23 x 96 sts/1131 total sts

START POSITION: Refer to Finishing Techniques: Making a Drawstring Bag (Cecille Border diagram)

FINISHED SIZE OF PROJECT: 10 x 4½in (25.5 x 11.5cm)

Model stitched by Krista West. ▸▸▸

Supplies

- One piece of 26ct Mikini in white, 5½ x 22in (14 x 57cm)

- DMC Floss:

  3012 khaki green medium, 4yds/3.7m (<1 skein)

  21 light alizarin, 3yds/2.8m (<1 skein)

  3857 rosewood dark, 3yds/2.8m (<1 skein)

  469 avocado green, 1yd/1m (<1 skein)

Finishing

To finish as shown, you will need one piece of lining fabric 22 x 5½in (57 x 14cm) and one drawstring cord 24in (61cm long); follow instructions for Making a Drawstring Bag (see Finishing Techniques).

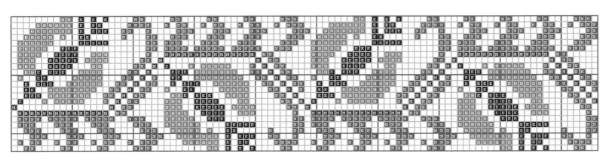

PRIMROSE BANDING

Garment Trim

☐ This project illustrates how a little bit of folk embroidery can be a beautiful addition to any garment. A traditional floral border is used as banding on the bodice of a child's pinafore but would be lovely as a pocket trim too.

SIZE OF STITCHED AREA: 1 x 4in (2.5 x 10cm)
STITCH COUNT: 15 x 59 sts/156 total sts
START POSITION: Center start (see Getting Started)
FINISHED SIZE OF PROJECT: Will vary depending on garment

*Model stitched by Krista West;
pinafore sewn by Josephine Breen.* ▸▸▸

Supplies

- One piece of 30ct linen in off-white, 10 x 12in (25.5 x 30cm)

- DMC Floss:
  21 light alizarin,
  2yds/1.8m (<1 skein)

  469 avocado green,
  1yd/1m (<1 skein)

  926 grey green medium,
  1yd/1m (<1 skein)

Finishing

To finish as shown, follow instructions for Making Bandings (see Finishing Techniques).

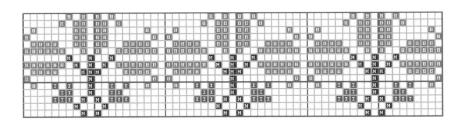

FINISHING TECHNIQUES

Traditional folk embroidery designs have been creating daily environments of color, charm, and cheer for millennia, and this section provides some classic ideas for how you, too, can make your folk embroideries into beautiful and useful items to enjoy every day. Finding new and innovative ways to incorporate folk embroidery into your daily life is part of the delight of this historic craft so I hope this is only a starting point for your creative makes. To finish your embroidery into one of the projects included here, you'll need an iron and ironing board or felt ironing pad, a pair of scissors, a ruler, pins and pincushion, sewing thread and a sharp sewing needle—a sewing machine, while not essential, can speed things up. Any additional tools required are noted at the beginning of each project.

MAKING TABLE MATS, SQUARES, AND RUNNERS

Many folk embroideries are simply hemmed for display on tables, shelves, or dressers. If you like to stitch on the go, a small table mat makes the ideal portable stitching project, while a table runner offers more design choice. You can finish your embroidery with a basic handsewn hem, but a traditional drawn thread hem is an elegant option and is my preferred choice.

Basic Hem

Note: These instructions are for making a finished 1in (2.5cm) hem but this can be adjusted to suit the project you are making.

1. Iron your finished embroidery lightly on the wrong side to remove any wrinkles, using the correct setting for the fiber content of your fabric and floss.

2. Starting in the middle of one side, use a ruler to measure 2in (5cm) out from the embroidered design and mark the thread at this point **(A)**.

3. Use a pin to gently pull the thread from the fabric to make a small loop. Placing your finger in the loop, use it to gently pull the thread out, gathering the fabric slightly in order to ease out the thread **(B)**. Completely remove the thread and discard.

4. Repeat steps 2 and 3 on the remaining sides to give you a drawn thread channel all the way around your embroidery **(C)**.

5. Using sharp scissors, trim the fabric along the drawn thread channel **(D)**.

6. Starting at one corner, fold the raw edge of the fabric over by 1in (2.5cm) and press **(E)**. Tuck the raw edge into the fold and press again to give you a double-fold hem. Repeat on the remaining sides, pinning every 6–8in (15.5–20cm) to hold the pressed hem in place **(F)**.

7. You will now create a miter at each corner, which reduces the bulk of the hem allowance and creates a neat finish. Open out the double-fold hem to reveal the pressed fold lines. Where the horizontal and vertical fold lines that are closest to the embroidered stitches intersect, fold the corner over at a 90-degree angle to form a triangle and press in place **(G)**. Trim the triangle to leave a ⅜in (1cm) seam allowance **(H)**. Keeping the triangle pressed in place, re-fold the hem into place, first on the horizontal fold **(I)** and then on the vertical fold **(J)**, to create the miter; pin in place **(K)**.

8. Repeat step 7 at each corner of your embroidery **(L)**.

9. To complete a basic hem, simply sew the pinned hem in place with a small whipstitch worked from the back of the embroidery around the entire perimeter, using a sharp needle and sewing thread.

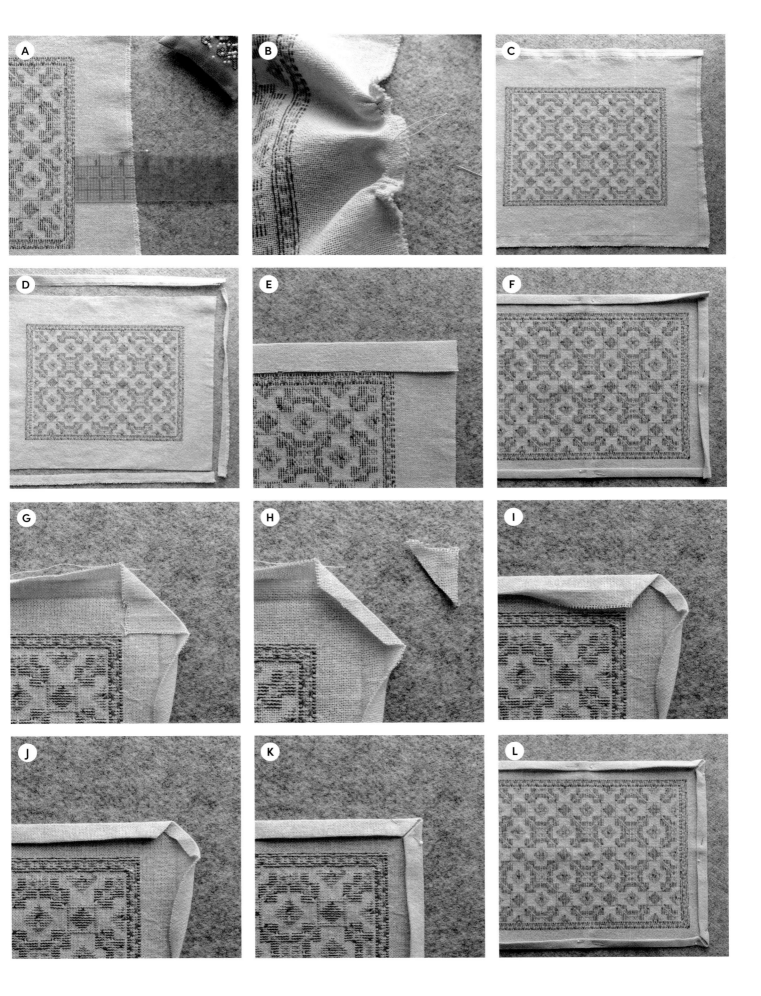

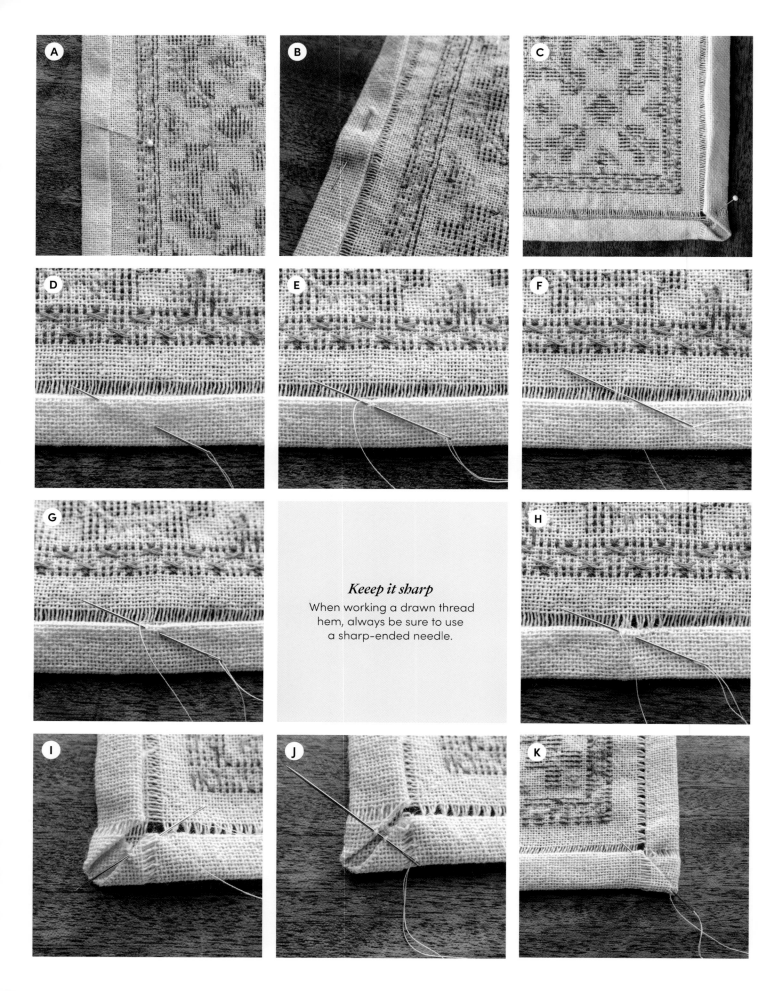

Keeep it sharp

When working a drawn thread hem, always be sure to use a sharp-ended needle.

Drawn Thread Hem

Drawing the threads

1. Follow Basic Hem steps 1–8, to the point where all four mitered corners have been pressed in place.

2. Now, working from the back side of the embroidery, determine which threads to remove. Working on each side in turn, count the number of threads starting from the edge of your embroidered design and ending at the hem fold. In the example shown here, there are 12 threads and we will be removing three threads, those threads closest to the hem fold and farthest away from the embroidered design, i.e. threads 10, 11, and 12, marking the thread that is furthest away with a pin **(A)**.

3. Repeat step 2 to count the threads on each side *before* you draw out the threads in order to make sure your hem allowance is even. For example, if in step 2 you have determined that threads 10, 11, and 12 should be pulled, count the threads of each side of the embroidery to make sure that threads 10, 11, and 12 are closest to the hem fold in each case. If they are not, you will need to adjust your hem fold slightly and press again.

4. Once you have determined the threads that need to be removed, pull each out as described in Basic Hem, step 3 **(B)**, removing one thread at a time and repeating on each side of the embroidery **(C)**.

Working the drawn thread hem stitch

5. Working with a single unknotted length of white sewing thread and a sharp sewing needle, and starting in the middle of one side on the back of your embroidery, pull the needle through the hem allowance about 1in (2.5cm) from where you want to begin stitching **(D)**. To anchor the thread, take two very small stitches in the hem fold only **(E)**.

6. Working right to left, put your needle in between two of the drawn threads, then bring it out three threads over in a "scooping" motion—you "scoop up" three threads and then bring the thread out without picking up any of the actual fabric, so that you are simply wrapping your sewing thread around three threads of the fabric **(F)**. Put your needle back into the hem fold at the first thread of your group of three threads and make a stitch (in the hem fold only) that starts at the right-hand thread of your group of three threads, coming out at the first thread of the next group of three threads. Pull gently but firmly so that the three threads form a little bar for your first drawn thread hem stitch **(G)**.

7. Continue to work drawn thread hem stitches in this manner up to the corner **(H)**. (As you reach a corner, you may need to wrap either two or four threads instead of the usual three.)

8. At the corner, float your thread through the hem fold and stitch the miter closed with a blind stitch **(I, J)**.

9. Once the corner has been stitched, float your thread through the hem fold to begin working the drawn thread hem stitch on the next side of the embroidery **(K)**.

10. When you have completed the drawn thread hem stitch on all four sides of the embroidery, secure the thread by taking one or two tack stitches through the hem fold, then sink your thread in the hem fold by about 1in (2.5cm) before pulling your needle out and trimming the thread. Press the hem lightly to set.

Variations on the drawn thread hem

Work drawn thread hem on two opposite sides only: Following the Drawn Thread Hem instructions, remove threads and work drawn thread hem stitch on two sides of the embroidery only, using whipstitch to secure the hem on the sides without drawn threads. The Linden Leaves Table Runner uses this variation, which allows the embroidery to go to the edge of the fabric.

Vary the depth of the hem allowance: If you would prefer a larger hem, allow 3–6in (7.5–15.5cm) on each side of the embroidery. The depth of the double-fold hem can also be increased if you desire.

Draw out more threads: You can remove additional threads to create a larger drawn thread hem. However, if you choose to do so, it is recommended that you work the drawn thread hem stitch on both sides of the drawn threads to create a more distinct "ladder" effect. To get the thread to the opposite side of the drawn threads, anchor the thread in the hem fold as described in step 5, then float the thread through one of the drawn thread bars to the other edge of the drawn threads.

Explore your drawn thread hem stitch options: The drawn thread hem technique described here is a great place to start, but if you desire a more intricate drawn thread hem with specialty stitches, you can research more complex stitches and techniques.

Note: If you would prefer to finish your table mat, square or runner by lining it, simply follow the instructions for Making a Wall Hanging, steps 1–6 only.

MAKING CUSHION COVERS

Many traditional folk embroideries were made into cushions and this finishing method provides a wonderfully cozy way to enjoy your handiwork. An embroidered cushion brings a lovely pop of color to your favorite chair, or display a group of cushions on a sofa for a boho vibe.

Basic Cushion Cover

There are many ways to make a cushion cover, but the envelope back method described here is an excellent choice as there are no zippers or closures to snag on the embroidery. Simple and quick, it can be sewn entirely by hand, although, a sewing machine does make the process faster. You will need a pillow form as well as fabric for the cushion backing.

1. Trim your embroidery to be a ½in (1.3cm) larger than your pillow form. For example, if you are using an 18 x 18in (46 x 46cm) pillow form, trim your embroidery to 18½ x 18½in (47.5 x 47.5cm).

2. Referring to the Cushion Cover Sizes table, cut two pieces of backing fabric for your pillow form size; for example, for an 18 x 18in (46 x 46cm) pillow form, cut two fabric pieces measuring 13 x 19in (33 x 48cm).

3. On one long edge of each piece of backing fabric, press over ½in (1.3cm) to the wrong side then ½in (1.3cm) again, to create a double-fold hem. Pin and stitch in place by hand or machine.

4. With right sides facing up, lay one backing piece on top of the other, so the hemmed edges overlap, to measure the same size as your trimmed embroidery. Baste (tack) the overlap in place **(A)**.

5. Place your cushion backing right side down, centered on top of your right side up embroidery and pin, trimming the backing to match as necessary. Then sew together using a ½in (1.3cm) seam allowance all the way around the edge. (I recommend stitching from the embroidery side so you can place the stitches along the counted thread fabric to keep the stitching lines straight and even. Trim corners to reduce bulk **(B)**.

6. Turn the cushion cover inside out, using a chopstick to gently ease out the corners **(C)**. Lightly press on front and back. Insert the pillow form and adjust the cushion back until it lays flat. Strike the cushion firmly against a table several times to help settle the pillow form into place **(D)**. If needed, lightly press the edges of the cushion cover.

Cushion Cover Sizes	
For pillow form size	*Cut backing fabric x 2*
12 x 12in (30 x 30cm)	9 x 13in (23 x 33cm)
14 x 14in (35.5 x 35.5cm)	10 x 15in (25.5 x 38cm)
16 x 16in (40.5 x 40.5cm)	12 x 17in (30 x 43cm)
18 x 18in (46 x 46cm)	13 x 19in (33 x 48cm)
20 x 20in (50 x 50cm)	14 x 21in (35.5 x 53cm)
24 x 24in (61 x 61cm)	18 x 25in (46 x 63.5cm)

Wrinkle free

After stitching your embroidery, press it with a medium iron to remove any creases before making it into your cushion cover.

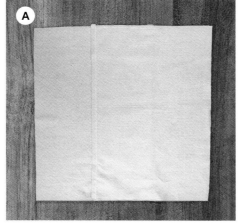

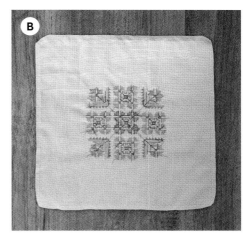

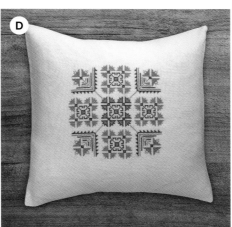

Plump pillows

Pillows look best when they are plump and to get this look, you need to make your cushion cover a little smaller than the pillow form!

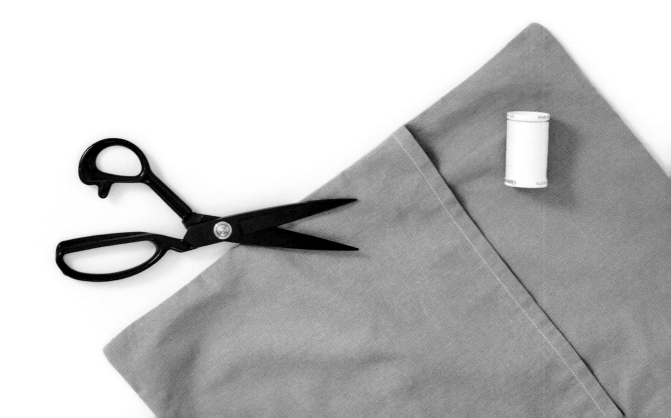

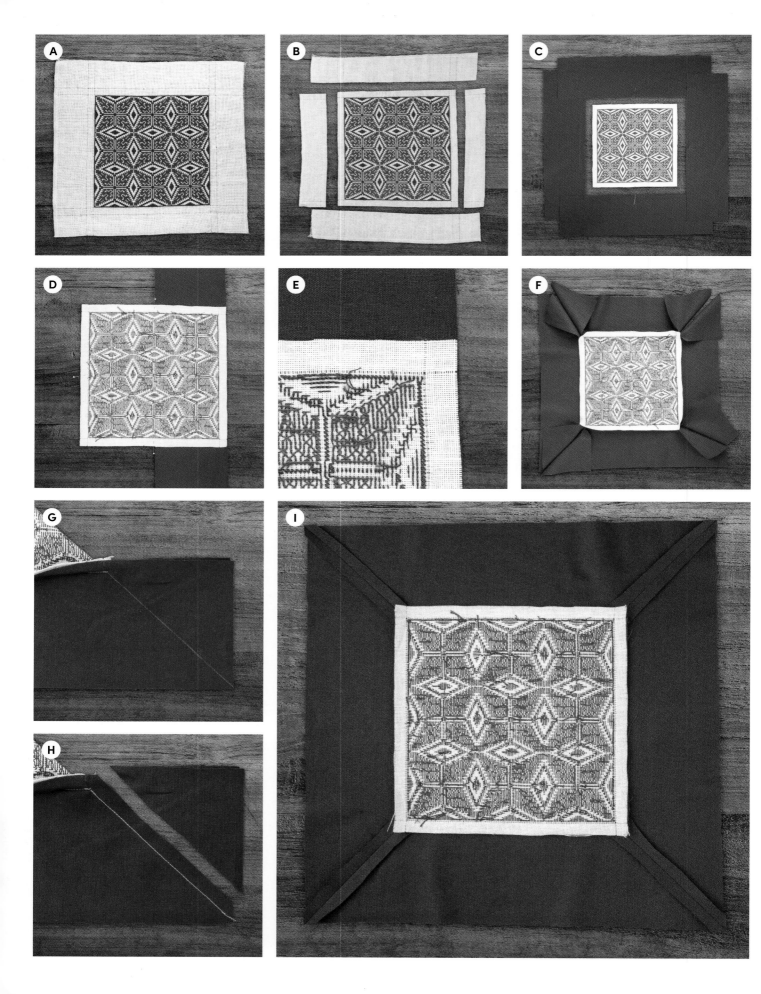

Cushion Cover with Mitered Border

For this variation of the envelope-backed cushion cover, the embroidery is inset within a mitered border of coordinating or contrasting fabric. This is a great way to show off a smaller piece of embroidery within a larger frame but beware, precision measuring is required!

1. Begin by preparing for the trimming of your embroidery, working on each side in turn. Referring to Making Table Mats, Squares, and Runners: Basic Hem, step 3, pull a thread at the edge of the embroidery, then measure ½in (1.3cm) out from the first pulled thread and pull out another thread, to give you two drawn thread channels all the way around your embroidery (**A**).

2. Trim your embroidery along the outer drawn thread channel, providing you with the ½in (1.3cm) seam allowance to sew the embroidery to the mitered borders in step 5 (**B**). *Note:* For the miters to work properly, the trimmed embroidery must be square. If your embroidered design is not perfectly square, do make sure the embroidery fabric is square once you have trimmed it.

3. To establish the size of the fabric pieces required for the mitered border, start by determining the difference between the width of your chosen pillow form size and the trimmed embroidery size, as follows:

*Pillow form width_____in/cm

**Embroidery width (inc. seam allowance)_____in/cm

Subtract * from **_____in/cm

Take this number and halve it, then add 1in (2.5cm) for seam allowances to give you the **width** of the border fabric pieces. The **length** will be the same size as the width of your pillow form plus ½in (1.3cm).

For example, for the Naxos Star Mitered Cushion, the calculation is as follows:

Pillow form width of 18in (46cm) **minus** embroidery width (inc. seam allowance) of 10in (25.5cm) **equals** 8in (20.5cm). Divide this number in half and add 1in

(2.5cm) for seam allowance: 4in + 1in (10cm + 2.5cm) = 5in (12.5cm) to give the width of the border fabric strips. So the size of the fabric pieces required for the mitered border strips for the Naxos Star Mitered Cushion is 5in (12.5cm) wide by 18½in (47.5cm) long.

4. Cut four fabric pieces to the dimensions required to make your cushion cover, as identified in step 3.

5. Mark the center of each side of your embroidery with a pin. Next, mark the center of each long edge of your border fabric strips by folding each in half and mark the fold with a pin (**C**).

6. Take one of your border strips and pin it to the embroidery, right sides together and matching up pins (**D**). With the embroidery on top, sew the border strip to the embroidery along the pulled thread channel, making sure to start and stop *exactly* at the corner of the pulled thread channel (**E**).

7. Repeat step 6 to sew a border strip to each side of the embroidery. Press the seam allowance towards the border strips; *do not* press the miters at the corners (**F**).

8. Now it's time to sew the miters in place, working on one corner at a time. Fold the embroidery in half diagonally, so right sides are together and the border strips are aligned. Mark a line from the place on the embroidery where the two pulled thread channels cross to the outer corner of the border strips (**G**). Sew along this line, backstitching at each end and taking care not to catch in any of the embroidery in the seam. Trim the seam allowance on the mitered border fabric to ½in (1.3cm) (**H**). Repeat on all four corners.

9. When all corners have been sewn and excess fabric trimmed away, press open the mitered seams then press the embroidery towards the mitered borders to complete the cushion cover front (**I**).

10. To make an envelope backing to complete the mitered cushion, see Basic Cushion Cover, steps 2–6.

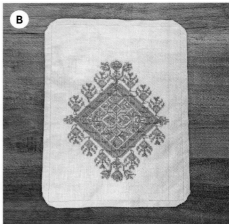

Textural appreciation

When an embroidery is displayed on a tapestry rod instead of being framed, you can more easily see the texture of the fabric and stitches.

Careful unpicking

When removing the stitches for the casing, use the seam ripper to rip one stitch at a time to prevent tearing your fabric.

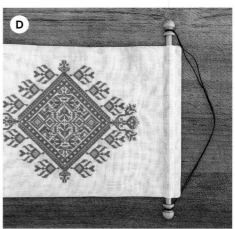

MAKING WALL HANGINGS

Many Greek homes have an embroidered wall hanging near the door to welcome guests with a cheery *"Kalimera!"* ("Good day!"). These can be hung on the wall, or on a freestanding display stand on a table. You'll need a lining fabric and a tapestry rod to complete this project.

1. Once your embroidery is complete, iron it lightly on the wrong side.

2. Determine the finished size of the hanging by pulling a thread channel all the way around your embroidered design to your desired measurements. For the Dodecanese Ornamental Wall Hanging, for example, this is as follows: 1in (2.5cm) away from the embroidered design on each side, 1½in (4cm) on the bottom edge and 3in (7.5cm) on the top edge. (Refer to Basic Hem, step 3 in Making Table Mats, Squares, and Runners for how to pull a thread.)

3. Now pull another thread channel exactly ½in (1.3cm) out from each of these pulled thread channels. Trim your embroidery along the second pulled thread channels.

4. Place your trimmed embroidery onto your chosen lining fabric and trim the lining fabric to the same size as your embroidery (A).

5. With your trimmed embroidery and your lining fabric right sides facing, sew together using the remaining pulled thread channel as your guide and leaving a 5in (13cm) opening along the bottom edge for turning. Trim corners to reduce bulk (B).

6. Turn right side out using a chopstick to ease out the corners, then press. Blind stitch the turning gap closed.

7. Now to make the casing for the tapestry rod: With the embroidered side facing you, sew a line of stitching ½in (1.3cm) away from the top edge. Then sew another line of stitching ¾in (2cm) below the first. Using a seam ripper, carefully remove a few stitches from the seam between these two rows of stitching to open up the casing (C), then slide the tapestry rod through it (D).

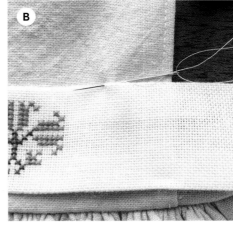

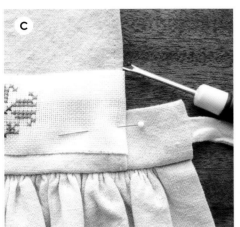

MAKING BANDINGS

Small bandings of folk embroidery can be used as an embellishment for any number of projects, from tote bags and towels, to curtains and clothes. A great way to use up leftover bits of fabric and floss, they are practical too, as your embroidery can be removed and reused as the garment or item wears out.

Note: If the item you plan to attach your banding to needs to be laundered, then pre-wash your embroidery before finishing it into banding.

1. Embroider your chosen border design on the evenweave fabric of your choice, leaving at least 2in (5cm) of fabric all around.

2. Trim your embroidery to your desired size allowing for an additional ½in (1.3cm) seam allowance all around, then press the seam allowance to the wrong side (A).

3. Sew the banding by hand to the project of your choice using small whip stitches (B).

4. If you are sewing banding to a made garment, you can use a seam ripper to carefully remove stitches from the item of clothing as needed in order to tuck the banding into the garment seam (C). Topstitch over the any existing topstitching lines by machine to blend with previous stitches (D).

MAKING A DRAWSTRING BAG

Small drawstring bags stitched with traditional designs are a delightful way to stay organized. I discovered this lined bag technique on one of my trips to Greece and I have been using it ever since! The instructions given are for making a small narrow bag ideal for storing pencils or your eyeglasses, but can easily be adapted to make a larger or wider bag.

1. Fold your evenweave fabric in half and mark the center with a pin or a bit of floss. Open out the fabric and begin stitching your design, positioning the embroidery so that it is ½in (1.3cm) to the left of the center of the fabric as shown in the Cecille Border diagram. (For the Oak Leaves Drawstring Bag, follow the Oak Leaves diagram to begin your embroidery 2½in (6cm) to the left of the center of the fabric.)

2. Determine the finished size of the bag by pulling a thread channel all the way around your embroidered design to your desired measurements. (Refer to Making Table Mats, Squares, and Runners: Basic Hem, step 3 for how to pull a thread.)

3. Now pull another thread channel exactly ½in (1.3cm) out from the first pulled thread channels, then trim your embroidery along the second pulled thread channels.

4. Place your trimmed embroidery onto your lining fabric and trim the lining fabric to the same size (A).

5. With your trimmed embroidery and your lining fabric right sides facing, sew together using a ¼in (6mm) seam allowance, leaving a 5in (13cm) opening on one long edge for turning. Trim corners to reduce bulk (B). Turn right side out, using a chopstick to gently ease out the corners, and press, making sure that the seam allowance on the turning gap is folded to the inside.

6. To make the casing for the drawstring, sew two parallel lines of stitching at each short end, with the first line of stitching just a little over 1in (2.5cm) away from the edge and the second line ½in (1.3cm) away from the edge (C), backstitching at the start and finish.

7. Using a seam ripper, carefully slit the stitches holding the embroidery to the lining in the seams between the two rows of stitching, working at each short end in turn, to open up the casing (see Making a Wall Hanging, step 7).

8. Fold the bag in half so that the lining is on the inside; pin, then sew the side seams together along the drawn thread channel, stitching from the bottom edge of the casing to the fold at the base of the bag (D). Press lightly.

9. Now thread the drawstrings through the casings. For this, you will need to cut two pieces of braided embroidery floss (or cord or ribbon) to a length of 24in (61cm) (for larger bags, use 36in/91cm lengths). Pin the end of one drawstring to a safety pin and feed it from right to left through the back casing then through the front casing from left to right, so that the tail ends are on the same side. Then feed the remaining drawstring through the opposite direction, to ensure the drawstring closes evenly from each side. Knot the two drawstrings at each end to finish (E).

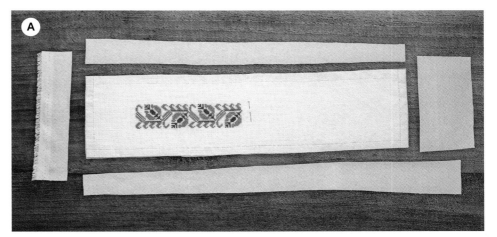

Drawn to it

For different cording options for your drawstrings, consider using velvet ribbon, grosgrain ribbon, or leather strips.

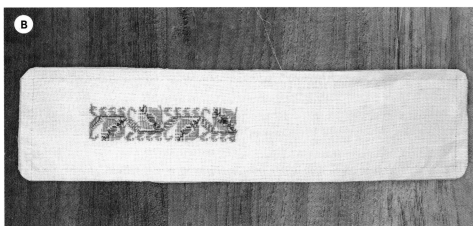

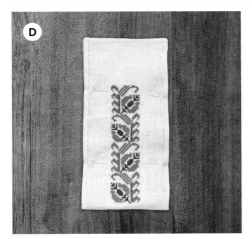

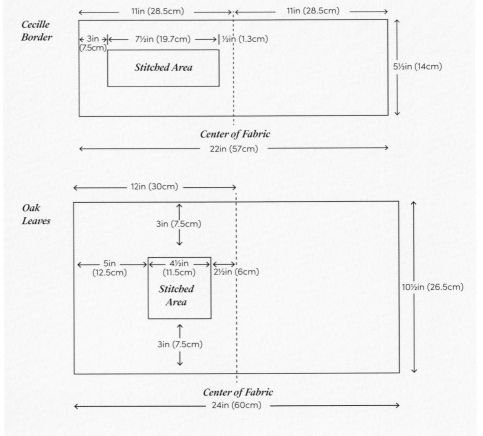

Cecille Border

11in (28.5cm) | 11in (28.5cm)

3in (7.5cm) | 7½in (19.7cm) | ½in (1.3cm)

Stitched Area

5½in (14cm)

Center of Fabric

22in (57cm)

Oak Leaves

12in (30cm)

3in (7.5cm)

5in (12.5cm) | 4½in (11.5cm) | 2½in (6cm)

Stitched Area

10½in (26.5cm)

3in (7.5cm)

Center of Fabric

24in (60cm)

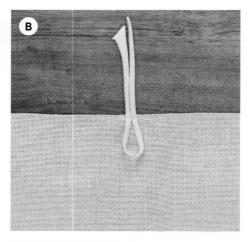

In the loop

An alternative option for making the loop for the button-and-loop closure would be simply to use a braided cord—a great way to use up your leftover floss.

More or less

You can use smaller borders to create an envelope bag for a smartphone or larger borders to create one for a laptop.

MAKING AN ENVELOPE BAG

This elegant, lined envelope bag has a button-and-loop closure. The measurements given can easily be adjusted to fit the dimensions of your tablet or a special notebook. You'll need a bias loop turner to make the loop, and a pretty button.

1. Once the embroidery is complete, iron it lightly on the wrong side. Trim your embroidered fabric to the desired width and height of your bag, *plus* approx. ½in (1.3cm) to each side for the seam allowance. For example, the bag I made has a finished size of 9½in (24cm) wide by 11in (28cm) high, so my trimmed fabric measured 10½in (24cm) by 12in (30.5cm). Cut a second piece of evenweave fabric to the same size for the bag back.

2. Sew the back of the bag to the embroidered bag front along the bottom edge, using a ½in (1.3cm) seam allowance. Press seam open.

3. Place your joined bag back/front onto your chosen lining fabric and trim the lining fabric to the same size (**A**).

4. Make the bias loop for the closure: cut one bias strip of fabric 5in (13cm) long and 1¼in (3.2cm) wide. Fold in half lengthwise and sew ⅛in (3mm) away from the fold. Trim the seam allowance to a scant ⅛in (3mm) and turn inside out using a loop turner. Position your loop (with the loop facing inwards) at the center of the top edge on the right side of the back of the bag (**B**).

5. With the joined bag back/front and lining fabric right sides facing, sew together using a ¼in (6mm) seam allowance, leaving a 4in (10cm) opening on one long edge for turning (**C**). Turn right side out, using a chopstick to gently ease out the corners, and press making sure that the seam allowance on the turning gap is folded to the inside.

6. Fold the bag in half so that the lining is on the inside, and sew the side seams together ¼in (6mm) from the edge, stitching from the top edge to the bottom fold. Press lightly.

7. Finally, sew the button to the top edge of the front of the bag to align with the loop (**D**, **E**).

DESIGN LIBRARY

The design library has many more folk embroidery designs for you to choose from. Here, you'll learn how to adapt these patterns to make your own folk embroidery masterpieces. Whether you already have an idea of what you would like to make—a cozy cushion cover for your sofa in a specific size, perhaps—or you're irresistibly drawn to stitch a motif but you're not sure what to make with it yet, you'll find all the information you need to continue your journey, learning how to adapt designs, sizes, and colors to develop projects that are uniquely yours.

Planning Your Folk Embroidery Project

Throughout history, folk embroidery designs have been passed from stitcher to stitcher, with the change of a color here or the use of a different layout there, with each embroiderer adding their own creativity and ingenuity to the newest version, which is then passed on to the next generation. Get ready to take your part in that long tradition.

CHOOSING YOUR FINISHED PROJECT

When designing your own folk embroideries, you will start by either choosing your finished project or choosing your design. Your choice of design will have an influence on what you make your finished stitching into. In these sketches, I'll recommend some classic design style layouts for some of the most popular projects but there are a few extra design ideas, too, to get you thinking creatively.

Table Runners

Rectangular in shape, table runners are a larger version of a table mat, but because of their larger size, there is more space to work with and therefore more design choices available.

Design Idea

Repeat a large single motif down the center and add a small coordinating border around the perimeter.

Allover

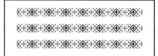

Small Borders

Centered Border

Perimeter Border

Double-Ended

Table Mats

Small embroidered mats are often seen in Mediterranean homes, displayed on a table with a family photo, an icon, or a candle placed on top.

Design Idea

Choose a double-ended border design, but work fewer repeats of the stylized motifs.

Allover

Large Single Motif

Centered Border

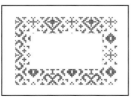

Perimeter Border

Table Squares

Table squares share similarities with cushion covers due to their square format, but they are often displayed in a diamond orientation with each corner of the square draped over the edge of a table. Perimeter border is the most common design style used for table squares.

Design Idea

Place a single motif in the center of a perimeter border.

Allover

Perimeter Border

Single Motif (centered)

Cushion Covers

Some of these suggested layouts are faster to stitch than others. You can produce a vibrant cushion in just a few weeks with centered border and single motif design styles, while allover or perimeter border designs require more stitching but yield a lavish result.

Design Idea

Place a centered border design off-center— either higher or lower.

Design Idea

Mirror a double-ended border across a cushion cover or table runner.

Perimeter Border

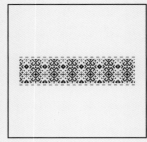

Centered Border

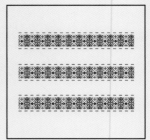

Small Borders

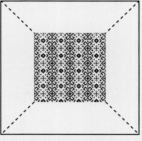

Allover with Mitered Border

Single Motif

Allover

Wall Hangings

The following design styles work well for wall hangings: allover, centered border (displayed vertically), small borders (in rows), and large single motifs. Due to the variety of sizes and finishes of tapestry rods widely available, it is easy to turn your stitching into a wall hanging any size you desire (see Finishing Techniques).

Bandings

For embellishments such as garment trims, the best design styles are single motifs or small borders.

Mixing and Matching Design Styles

Blending designs and influences is a fundamental part of folk embroidery. Maritime trading over the centuries has promoted cultural interchange by bringing textiles, pattern books, new fashions, and even skilled artisans from country to country. This is why a vintage Greek folk embroidery might have a French feel, or a Venetian pattern look very Byzantine. In the Design Library, I have included a wide variety of designs from many lands so you too can carry on this wonderful tradition of mixing and matching. Consider combining a large geometric border with a small floral one, or adding a delicate tiny border to a single motif—however you choose to mix and match, know that you are in good company with stitchers throughout the generations!

CALCULATING YOUR FABRIC SIZE

Once you've selected your design and decided on your finished project, the next step is to calculate the size required for your stitching fabric following either the simple start method or the detailed start method.

Simple Start Method

A simplified method of calculating your design fabric, this will not be as exact as the step-by-step calculations required for the detailed start, but it's easier and quicker just so long as you don't mind a bit of variation in the finished size of your project.

Step One: Add finishing allowance to your approximate finished project size

Starting with an estimated size for your finished project, add a generous finishing allowance as follows:

For all design styles: Add 3in (7.5cm) to EACH side.

For example: If I want a finished cushion cover 18 x 18in (46 x 46cm), I add 3in (7.5cm) to each side to give a design fabric size of 24 x 24in (61 x 61cm).

Step Two: Begin stitching

For Allover, Perimeter Border, or Double-Ended Designs: Begin stitching your design 2in (5cm) in from each corner, then work your repeat motif until you have at least 2–3in (5–7.5cm) of space on each side of the embroidery.

For Centered Border, Single Motif, or Small Border Designs: Begin stitching in the center of your fabric from the center of your design, working outwards until you have stitched your desired area, making sure to leave at least 2–3in (5–7.5cm) of space on each side of the embroidery.

Detailed Start Method

This method ensures you end up with a folk embroidery project that is the exact size you want it to be. I have provided a Design Worksheet that you can fill in at the start of most projects (see Variations According to Design Style for exceptions). Just follow the step-by-step advice and my working example given below.

Step One: Count the repeat motif

Choosing a design from the Design Library—count the stitches horizontally and vertically in the black box that identifies the repeat motif. Make a note of these on your Design Worksheet.

For example, for my working example I have chosen a design with a repeat motif that is 12 stitches horizontally and 10 stitches vertically.

Step Two: Calculate size of stitched area and stitch count

For your first calculation—choose the approximate size you would like your finished project to be and subtract 2in (5cm)—(1in/2.5cm per side) to determine the Stitched Area:

For example, I have chosen to make a table runner with an approximate finished size of 8in (20cm) wide by 14in (35.5cm) long, so my calculations look like this:

Approx. Finished Project Width: 8in (20cm) less 2in (5cm) = 6in (15cm) wide (Stitched Area)

Approx. Finished Project Length: 14in (35.5cm) less 2in (5cm) = 12in (30.5cm) long (Stitched Area)

For your second calculation—you will need to choose what evenweave fabric you will be stitching on to, in order to record its stitch count. As all projects in this book are stitched over two threads, a 30ct fabric results in 15 stitches to the inch (2.5cm), a 26ct fabric results in 13 stitches to the inch (2.5cm), and so on. So, take your Stitched Area and multiply by the fabric stitch count (i.e. the number of stitches per inch) to determine the approximate Stitch Count (of Stitched Area):

For example, I am using 30ct linen for my table runner so my calculations look like this:

Stitched Area: 6in (15cm) wide multiplied by 15 sts per inch = 90 sts wide

Stitched Area: 12in (30.5cm) long multiplied by 15 sts per inch = 180 sts long

Therefore the Stitch Count of my Stitched Area is 90 x 180 sts

Step Three: Calculate exact size of stitched area for fabric size excluding finishing allowance

First, you need to calculate how many repeat motifs can be stitched across your fabric by dividing your stitch count for the stitched area by the stitch count for your repeat motif. Then you ROUND UP the calculated numbers and multiply them by the stitch count of your repeat motif to get the stitch count of your adjusted stitched area.

For example, the stitch count for the stitched area of my table runner is 90 x 180 sts and the stitch count for my repeat motif is 12 sts horizontally and 10 sts vertically, so I will fill in my Design Worksheet as follows:

Stitch Count (of Stitched Area) Width: 90 sts divided by 12 sts per repeat motif (horizontal) = 7.5 total repeats

I then round this number up and multiply it by the horizontal stitch count of my repeat motif to get the adjusted Stitched Area Width:

8 total repeats multiplied by 12 sts per repeat motif = 96 total width stitches

Stitch Count (of Stitched Area) Length: 180 sts divided by 10 sts per repeat motif (vertical) = 18 total repeats

I then round this number up and multiply by the vertical stitch count of my repeat motif to get the adjusted Stitched Area Length:

18 total repeats multiplied by 10 sts per repeat motif = 180 total length stitches

So my adjusted Stitched Area Stitch Count is: 96 sts wide by 180 sts long

Then you need to take the adjusted stitched area stitch count and convert it back into inches (centimeters) so you can calculate the finishing allowance in Step Four: Add Finishing Allowance more easily.

For example, my Stitch Count Width is 96 sts divided by 15 sts per inch (2.54 centimeters) = 6.4in (16.25cm) and my Stitch Count Length is 180 sts divided by 15 sts per inch = 12in (30cm)

Rounding these numbers up to the nearest full inch, my Fabric Size Excluding Finishing Allowance is: 7in (18cm) wide by 12in (30cm) long

Step Four: Add finishing allowance

The final step is to add additional fabric for the finishing allowance, i.e. the extra fabric needed for hemming, sewing, or otherwise finishing your project. Once you have calculated this, you will know exactly how much fabric you need for your project and where to begin stitching. It is always better to have more finishing allowance than less, so when in doubt add extra!

For example, for my table runner, I will fill in the Design Worksheet as follows:

Stitched Area Width: 7in (18cm) PLUS 4in (10cm) finishing allowance = 11in (28cm)

Stitched Area Length: 12in (30cm) PLUS 4in (10cm) finishing allowance = 16in (40cm)

So the fabric size including finishing allowance that I require is 11in (28cm) wide by 16in (40cm) long.

Variations According to Design Style

Centered Border Table Runner or Cushion Cover

In Step Four of the Detailed Start Method, keep the finishing allowance on short edges to the standard 2in (5cm) per side/4in (10cm) total but add additional finishing allowance to the long edges as follows:

Centered Border Table Runner— Allow 5in (13cm) per side/10in (25.5cm) total on the long edges.

Centered Border Cushion Cover— allow 6in (15cm) per side/12in (30cm) total on the long edges.

Single Motif Cushion Cover

There is no need complete the Design Worksheet for most single motifs stitched as a cushion cover; simply choose the size of fabric you would like for your cushion cover (a good default is 18 x 18in/46 x 46cm), then begin stitching the motif in the center.

Small Borders Table Mat, Table Runner, or Cushion Cover

When calculating the vertical repeat motif, I'd recommend counting the stitches of your small borders and adding the unstitched stitches between them, treating them as one large border.

For example, if you work three rows of a small border that is 12 stitches vertically with 10 stitches in between, your total vertical repeat would be calculated as follows: 12 small border sts plus 10 blank sts plus 12 small border sts plus 10 blank stitches plus 12 small border sts = 56 sts.

Alternatively, you can simply choose your fabric size and begin working your first small border design in the center, adding additional small borders to either side as you have room.

DESIGN WORKSHEET

Please refer to Variations According to Design Style for any necessary revisions to this model.

A printable version of this worksheet is available to download from: www.bookmarkedhub.com.

*The default finishing allowance is 2in (5cm) per side, or 4in (10cm) per width or length. This means that stitching will start 2in (5cm) in from each corner.

If you want a larger finishing allowance, simply increase the finishing allowance accordingly. For example, if I wanted a deeper hem, I would allow 6in (15cm) of finishing allowance for the width and 6in (15cm) of finishing allowance for the length (i.e. 3in/7.5cm per side).

Step One: Count the Repeat Motif

Repeat Motif: ☐ stitches horizontally ☐ stitches vertically

. . . .

Step Two: Calculate Size of Stitched Area and Stitch Count

First calculation (Stitched Area):

Approx. Finished Project Width: ☐ in/cm less 2in (5cm) = ☐ in/cm wide (Stitched Area)

Approx. Finished Project Length: ☐ in/cm less 2in (5cm) = ☐ in/cm long (Stitched Area)

. . . .

Second calculation (Stitch Count of Stitched Area):

Stitched Area: ☐ inches wide multiplied by ☐ sts per inch (2.54 centimeters) = ☐ sts wide

Stitched Area: ☐ inches long multiplied by ☐ sts per inch (2.54 centimeters) = ☐ sts long

Stitch Count (of Stitched Area): ☐ sts wide by ☐ sts long

. . . .

Step Three: Calculate Exact Size of Stitched Area for Fabric Size Excluding Finishing Allowance

Stitch Count (of Stitched Area) Width: ☐ sts divided by ☐ sts per Repeat Motif (horizontal) = ☐ total repeats

Round this number up and then multiply by sts per Repeat Motif to get adjusted Stitched Area Width:

☐ total repeats multiplied by ☐ sts per Repeat Motif = ☐ sts (adjusted)

Stitch Count (of Stitched Area) Length:

☐ sts divided by ☐ sts per Repeat Motif (vertical) = ☐ total repeats

Round this number up and then multiply by sts per Repeat Motif to get adjusted Stitched Area Length:

☐ total repeats multiplied by ☐ sts per Repeat Motif = ☐ sts (adjusted)

Adjusted Stitched Area Stitch Count is: ☐ sts wide by ☐ sts long

. . . .

Now take the adjusted Stitched Area Stitch Count and calculate back into inches (centimeters) :

Stitch Count Width ☐ sts divided by ☐ sts per inch (2.54 centimeters) = ☐ in (cm)

Stitch Count Length ☐ sts divided by ☐ sts per inch (2.54 centimeters) = ☐ in (cm)

. . . .

Round these numbers up to the nearest full inch to get Fabric Size

Excluding Finishing Allowance: ☐ in (cm) wide by ☐ in (cm) long

. . . .

Step Four: Add Finishing Allowance

Stitched Area Width: ☐ in (cm) PLUS 4in (10cm)* finishing allowance = ☐ in (cm)

Stitched Area Length: ☐ in (cm) PLUS 4in (10cm)* finishing allowance = ☐ in (cm)

Fabric Size Including Finishing Allowance: ☐ in (cm) wide by ☐ in (cm) long

Using the Design Library Charts

The charts are presented in the six design style sections—Allover, Perimeter Border, Centered Border, Single Motif, Double-Ended, and Small Borders. You can switch out designs from the library for those used to make the Essential Projects, or, following the advice in Planning Your Folk Embroidery Project, create projects of your own.

REPEAT MOTIFS

You will notice that on the majority of the charts there is a black box around a section of the design. This is the "repeat motif," the basic unit that you will stitch repeatedly to complete your design. You will use the stitch count of the repeat motif (i.e. the number of stitches the motif takes up horizontally and vertically) to finalize the finished size of your project (see Detailed Start Method in Planning Your Folk Embroidery Project).

Backstitch Outlining

A few of the charted designs also feature a backstitch outlining stitch for some areas of the pattern and this is shown with solid lines of color. The backstitch outlines, just like the cross stitches, are worked over two threads of the fabric using two strands of DMC floss (or one strand of Appletons crewel wool). In these charts, the backstitches are worked either vertically or horizontally, as follows: with the needle at the front of the embroidery, count over two threads and take your needle through the fabric to make your first stitch; then count over another two threads to bring your needle back out to the front of the fabric; take the needle back down through the fabric where you ended the previous stitch to complete the second stitch; now bring the needle back out two threads of the fabric from the last completed stitch and continue in this manner.

....

Tip

If you need a reminder on how to work from charts, see Getting Started—Step Three: Begin Stitching.

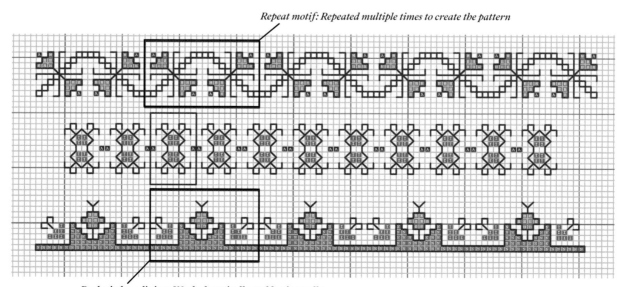

Repeat motif: Repeated multiple times to create the pattern

Backstitch outlining: Worked vertically and horizontally over 2 fabric threads with 2 strands of floss

Creating with color

The colors of the charted designs are simply suggestions and you can experiment with changing floss colors with others from my color palette. Let's take as an example, one of the Essential Projects, the Naxos Stars Cushion Cover. The charted design uses the red colorway traditional to the embroideries of the Greek island of Naxos, and I have used DMC 355 and 3857. However, this design would look equally compelling stitched in a blue colorway (using DMC 926 and DMC 924), or in a gold colorway (using DMC 733 and DMC 730).

In fact, there's nothing to stop you from choosing a different color palette altogether, using brighter shades if you'd prefer them to my more subtle tones, for example. And as well as the colors of the floss you are using, there's fabric color choice to consider too. Here are a few more ideas to get you thinking:

- A monochromatic (single-colored) single motif design can look great stitched with a light floss color on a darker fabric, such as ivory on a deep red for instance.

- Polychromatic (many-colored) allover, perimeter border, or double-ended designs take on a truly traditional folk look when stitched in a single color—such as red, black, or navy—on a light-colored fabric.

- Try stitching a monochromatic small border in multiple hues of the same shade for an ombre effect.

- Choose a darker colored fabric for a perimeter border design, where the center of the fabric is unstitched, to provide extra interest—for a Scandinavian vibe, use a deep blue fabric and stitch in white.

- Emphasize the contrast between a centered border design and the unworked fabric at top and bottom of the stitched panel—red and black floss on a bright white fabric has a Ukrainian feel.

DESIGN LIBRARY MASTER KEY

I have used my palette of 14 DMC floss colors for the design library charts, using just five of those colors for backstitch outlining on some of the charted designs. Refer to the master key when working the designs.

	Key Cross Stitch with 2 strands	
A	DMC 3787	brown grey dark
B	DMC 3032	mocha brown medium
C	DMC 730	olive green very dark
D	DMC 733	olive green medium
E	DMC 3857	rosewood dark
F	DMC 815	garnet medium
G	DMC 355	terra cotta dark
H	DMC 21	light alizarin
K	DMC 924	grey green very dark
I	DMC 926	grey green medium
J	DMC 598	turquoise light
L	DMC 3810	turquoise dark
M	DMC 469	avocado green
N	DMC 3012	khaki green medium
	Key Backstitch (B/S) with 2 strands	
	DMC 3787	B/S ————
	DMC 730	B/S ————
	DMC 733	B/S ————
	DMC 3857	B/S ————
	DMC 924	B/S ————

ALLOVER DESIGNS

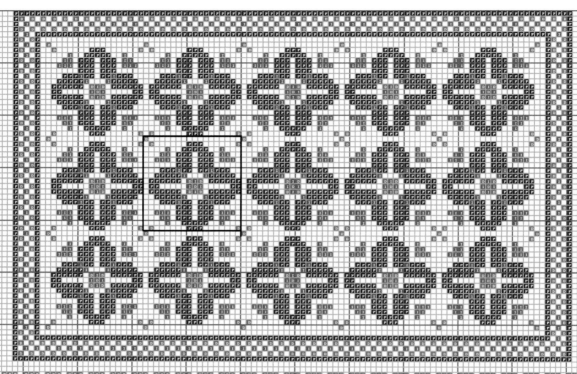

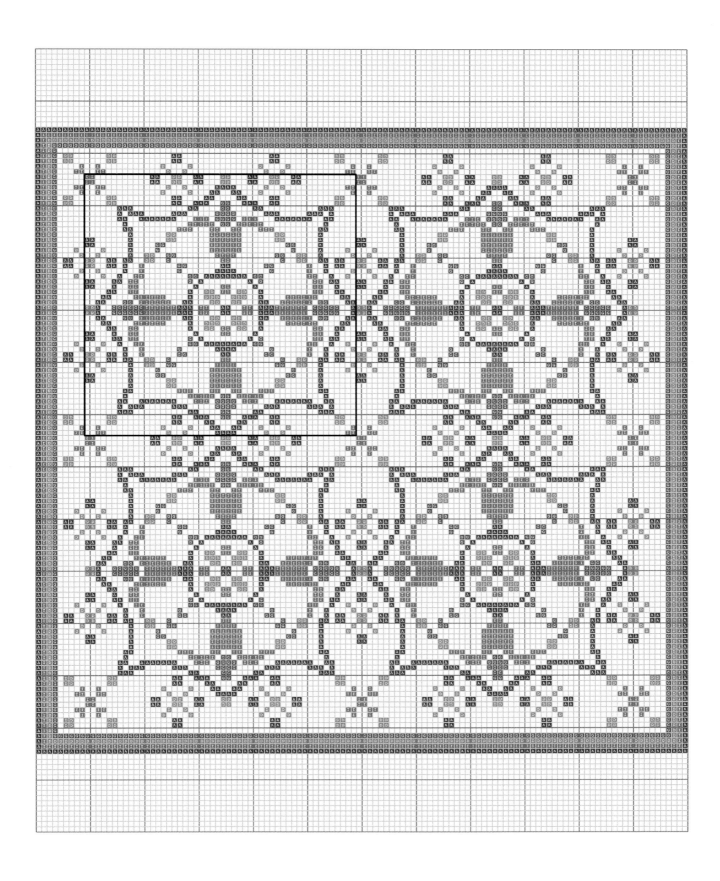

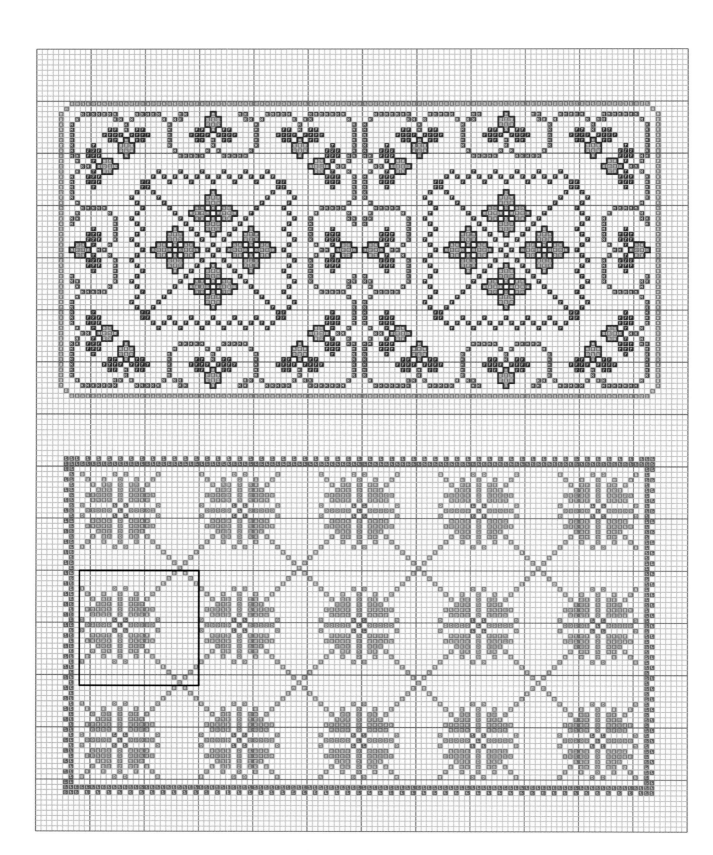

CENTERED BORDER DESIGNS

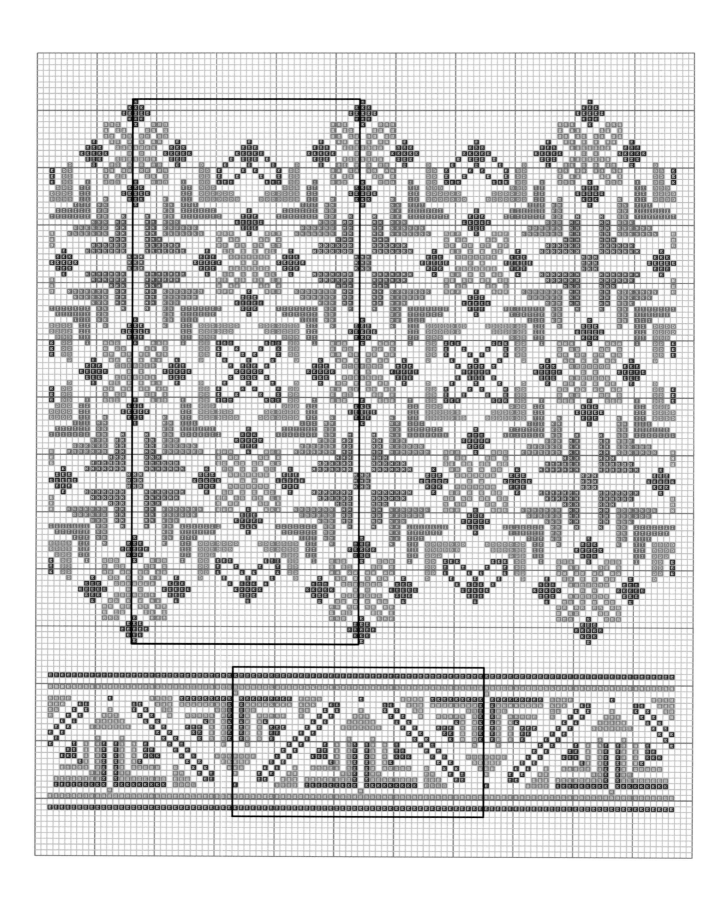

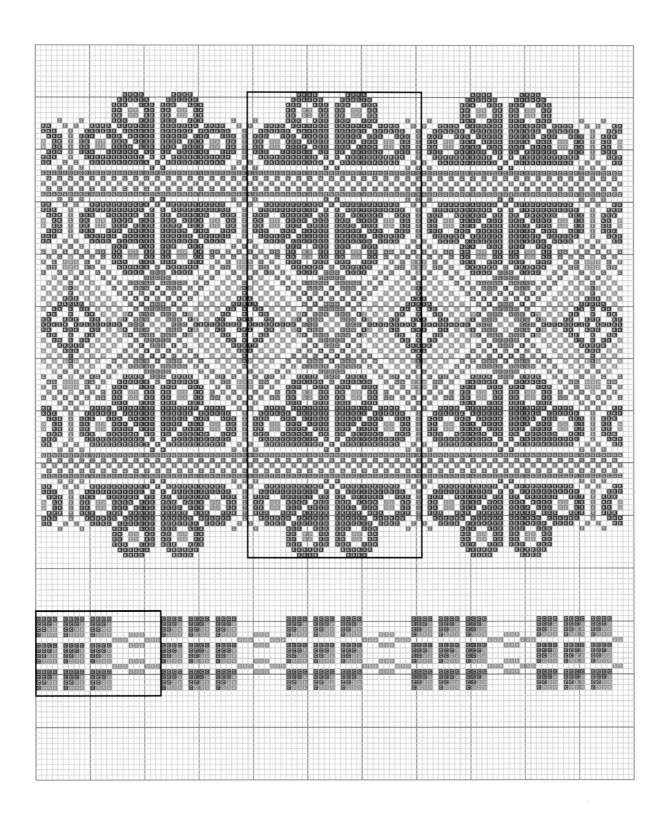

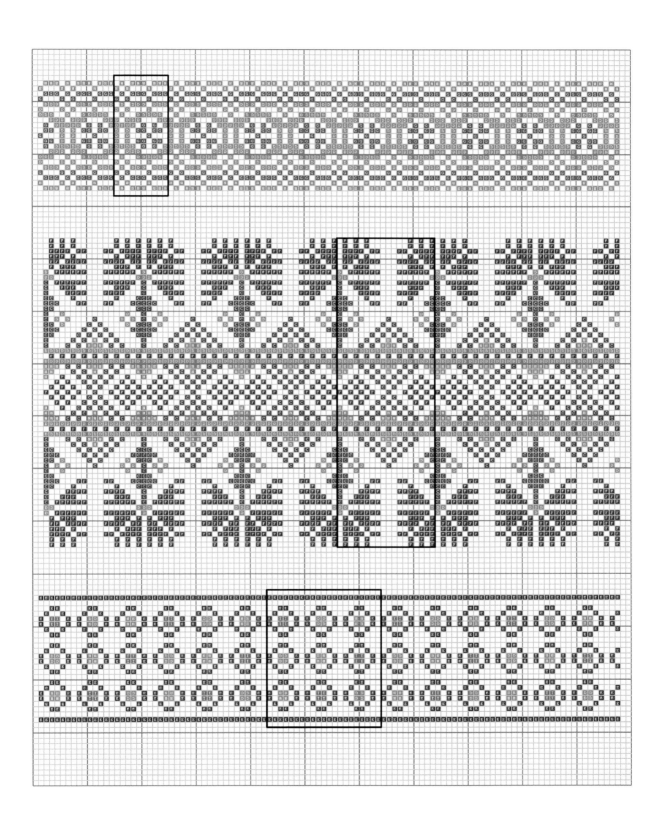

Centered Border Designs · Design Library ✳ 117

DOUBLE-ENDED DESIGNS

SINGLE MOTIF DESIGNS

PERIMETER BORDER DESIGNS

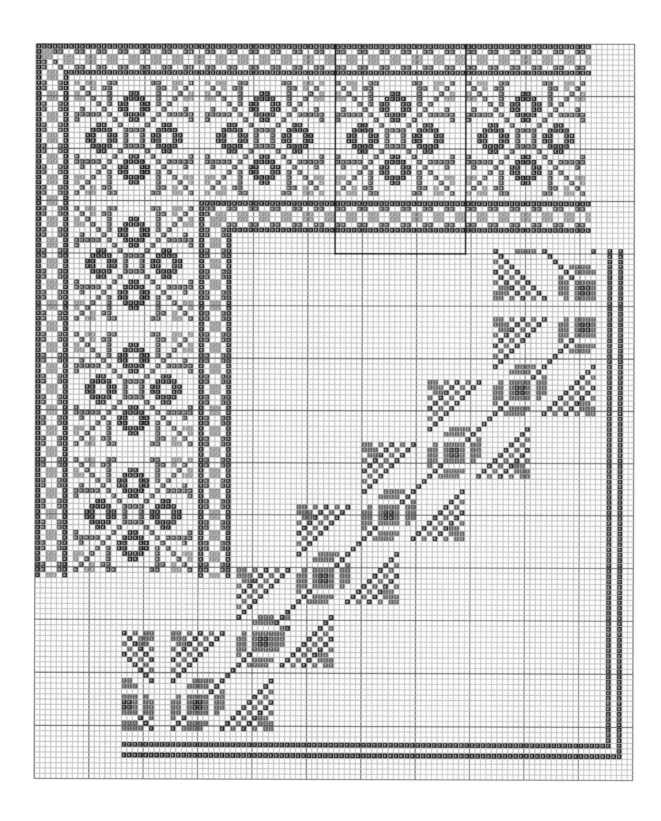

SMALL BORDER DESIGNS

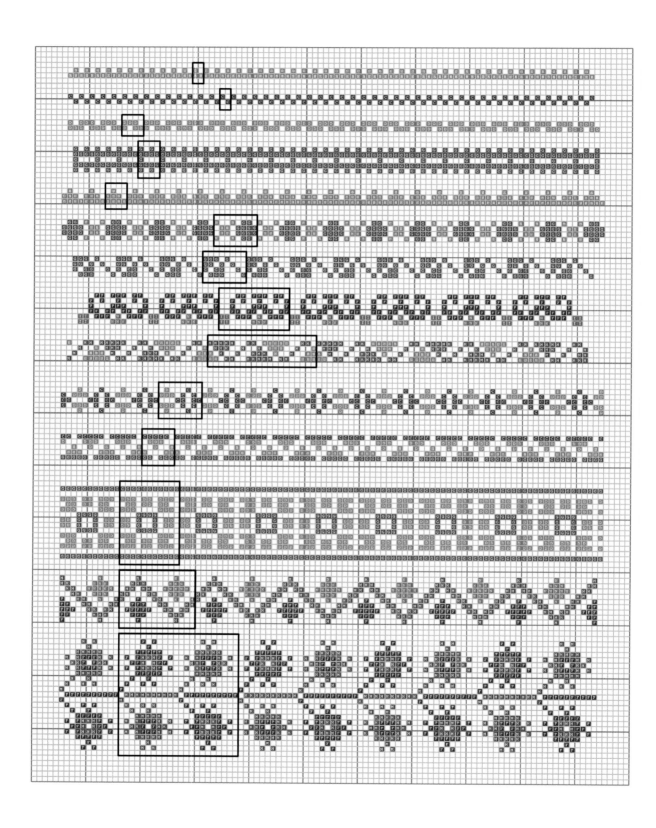

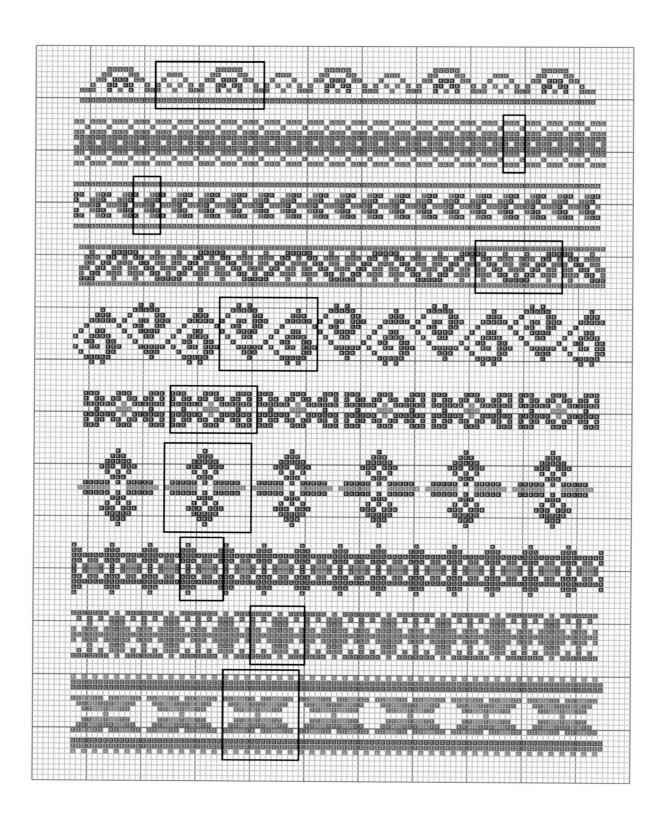

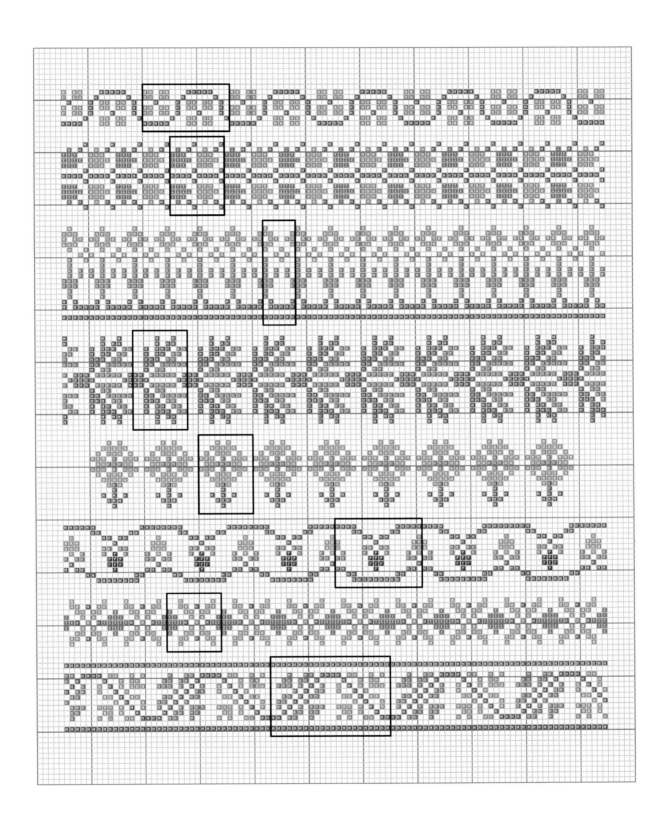

About the Author

Krista West delights in bringing ancient beauty to the modern world with embroidery designs inspired by traditional Mediterranean folk textiles. Introduced to traditional folk embroidery on one of her trips to Greece, she fell in love with the vibrant colors and historic motifs, and began stitching textiles for her own home. She quickly realized there was still much interest in this historic craft and she opened Avlea Folk Embroidery to share the beauty of folk embroidery. She happily spends her days in the workshop of her 1923 home in Salem, Oregon, designing patterns and making kits for customers and shops around the world. See her work at www.avleaembroidery.com, and follow her on YouTube and Instagram (@kristamwest).

Suppliers

Avlea Folk Embroidery

www.avleaembroidery.com

Appletons Crewel Wools

www.appletons.org.uk

Herrschners (DMC floss)

www.herrschners.com

Acknowledgments

I count myself a fortunate member of the worldwide folk embroidery community, a group of stitchers who, in addition to their enthusiasm for historical stitching, are amazingly kind and generous. I am grateful for the generosity and talents of Cindy Russell, Elizabeth Ostler, Maria Armstrong, Pamela Filbert, Rachael Marks, and Debera Mahassos, all of whom helped stitch samples for this book. I am also deeply grateful to my assistant, Pamela Filbert, who kept the Avlea workshop humming along so I could write and stitch for this book. I'd also like to thank Jim Tullin of WinStitch software for all of his help with charting.

Finally, I am deeply grateful for the love and support of my partner, Alban, and my daughter, Georgia, who were willing to listen to all things folk embroidery and make dinner when I forgot!

Index